"You cannot teach a man anything,
you can only help him to find it for himself."
- Galileo Galilei

©2021 Catherine Fet · North Landing Books · All Rights Reserved

*1453 – The Fall of Constantinople*

The Renaissance is a period of European history between the Middle Ages and the modern era, covering the 15th and 16th centuries. *Renaissance* is a French word which means 'rebirth.' The Renaissance was an era of rebirth, the rediscovery, of the culture of classical antiquity – ancient Greece and Rome, which had been nearly forgotten during the Dark and Middle Ages. It included a rediscovery of the pre-Christian idea of humanism – the focus on the perspective of man, rather than God – a philosophy that was grounded in everyday reality rather than in theology. The idea of humanism is best expressed in the words of the ancient Greek philosopher Protagoras, "Man is the measure of all things." How did it happen that the cultures of ancient Greece and Rome, the foundation of Western civilization, were suddenly rediscovered during the Renaissance?

By the 13th century there was a sense of stagnation in European thought, science, and art. Creative minds looked for new ideas to break away from the worldview of the Middle Ages. Scholars dug deeper into the libraries of European monasteries and universities, where they found Latin and Greek books by classical authors. Many ancient scrolls were brought to Italy from Constantinople, the capital of Byzantium, which was under attack by the Muslim Ottoman Turks. Some Byzantine scholars moved to Italy and taught Greek, spreading appreciation for classical philosophy, history, and literature – now called the *humanities*.

The term *humanities* came from the Latin word *humanitas* – human nature, civilization, and civilized conduct. Italian humanists borrowed it from Roman politician and author Cicero who used it to describe the skills of a wise leader. In 1453 the Muslims conquered and sacked Constantinople. A flood of Christian refugees arrived in Italy, bringing with them their libraries, higher standards of education, and knowledge of their ancient heritage.

After the invention of the movable type printing press by Gutenberg around 1456, the works of ancient Greek and Roman authors appeared in print, and for the first time became available to a wider circle of readers. Previously unseen ancient Roman sculptures and frescoes were unearthed and imitated by artists, and the classical architecture of Roman ruins was studied and appreciated. Rediscovered knowledge of ancient Greek scientists helped overturn medieval beliefs about the universe and develop the scientific method.

The medieval family structure where women didn't have any voice of their own was now in question as well. Ancient imperial Roman law allowed women to own and inherit property, required a woman's consent for marriage, and gave women who had three children complete financial and legal independence. As knowledge of the ancient world grew, so did the interest in more freedoms.

This spirit of humanism and renewal touched the world of Christian thought. The church had taught that the Earth was flat. But the voyages of Vasco da Gama, Columbus, and other explorers showed that it was round. If the church was proved wrong in one belief, could it be wrong in others as well? Many Catholic scholars began speaking up against church teachings and practices that they felt were outdated or self-serving. Demanding reform to the Church, they started the Reformation that split the new Protestant movement away from the Catholic Church.

The Renaissance first began in the Italian city-states of Florence and Venice, wealthy centers of commerce that could afford brand-new intellectual and artistic projects. From Italy the ideas and spirit of the Renaissance spread across the whole of Europe. The Black Death, a deadly pandemic that hit Europe from 1348 to 1350, killed so many people that the price of food and land fell, while the price of labor grew. As a result, a middle class – the class of skilled professionals and business owners – started to emerge in European cities, and more people sought education. The growing use of firearms in Europe in the middle of the 14th century changed the art of war and destroyed the status of knights. Knights were replaced by foot soldiers with guns. Castles became useless, chivalry was gone, the family bonds and class structure of the medieval society crumbled. The transition to the modern world was under way.

# Lorenzo the Magnificent
## 1449 – 1492

Lorenzo de' Medici, also known as Lorenzo the Magnificent, came from an influential family of Italian traders and bankers. His grandfather, Cosimo de' Medici was the first in his family to run both the Medici Bank and the government of Florence. Lorenzo received a brilliant education, tutored by stars of Florentine humanist elite, including John Argyropoulos, a Greek bishop and scholar, who was a refugee from Constantinople. As a teenager, fluent in Latin and Greek, Lorenzo started writing poetry, and showed great appreciation for the arts. Growing up, he enjoyed the typical activities of wealthy Florentine kids – jousting, hunting, falconry, and horse racing. But when he was 16 he also started going on diplomatic missions on behalf of his family.

In 1469 his father died and, at the age 21, Lorenzo took over the government of Florence. He ran it with an iron hand, with the help of his mother, Lucrezia, and his brother Giuliano. The Medici did not rule Florence directly. Instead they planted their own people in the city council. During Lorenzo's rule Florence flourished like never before, but its citizens had no political freedom whatsoever. All the power in the city belonged to Lorenzo who enjoyed splendid titles, the flattery of politicians and artists, wore stunning gilded robes, and lived in a magnificent palace.

Lorenzo could be ruthless. In the Italian town of Volterra they discovered alum, a chemical compound, that was used in glass-making and other industries. Until then alum was found only on territories under Turkish control. The citizens of Volterra first asked the Medici Bank to fund their mining work, but soon, realizing how valuable alum was, tried to cut out the Medici, and organized a rebellion. Furious, Lorenzo hired an army of mercenaries who sacked and burned Volterra. Hearing of the mercenaries' cruelties in Volterra, Lorenzo rushed there with apologies, but the blood of innocent citizens forever remained a horrific stain on his reputation.

Just like ancient Roman leaders who bought the support of their citizens with endless festivals, chariot races, and gladiator games, Lorenzo started his rule with an explosion of free entertainment for the crowds. And he was successful in keeping his subjects distracted and uninterested in public affairs. He paid the best artists to design masks, costumes, and decorate floats for masquerades and holiday processions. He wrote poetry for every occasion and personally participated in every spectacle.

Each generation of the Medici family had to confront conspiracies and murder plots staged by their rivals. In 1478 a conspiracy against Lorenzo was organized by the Pazzi family, a wealthy and proud Florentine clan who had been denied public offices and honors by the Medici. First the Pazzi got the support of Pope Sixtus IV, a corrupt and tyrannical ruler. Pope Sixtus had 6 nephews, all greedy and talentless individuals. He gave four of them well-paying bishops' jobs in the church, and the Pazzi promised the pope to bring Florence under his control and employ the rest of his nephews.

With the blessing of the Pope, the conspirators arrived at a banquet held by Lorenzo at his villa. Their plan was to murder Lorenzo and his brother Giuliano during the banquet. However Giuliano didn't show up, and the Pazzi changed their plan. They wanted both brothers dead.

*A portrait of Giuliano de' Medici by Sandro Boticelli; below: 'Adoration of the Magi' by Sandro Boticelli includes a portrait of 16-year-old Lorenzo with his horse.*

*'Madonna of the Magnificat' by Sandro Boticelli is a portrait of Lorenzo's mother, Lucrezia, with her children. Lorenzo holds a pot of ink.*

The next morning was Easter Sunday. Lorenzo came to High Mass at the city cathedral. And so did the assassin hired by the Pazzi. But the spiritual power of the mass awakened the conscience of the would-be killer, and he refused to commit the murder. One of the Pazzi, a priest at the cathedral, stepped in, ready to murder the Medici. But there was yet another problem. Giuliano was missing again! He had suffered a knee injury and stayed in bed. Without hesitation, the Pazzi went to Giuliano's house and offered to carry him to the cathedral!

When both Medici brothers were standing by the altar at the cathedral, the cardinal who was officiating the mass, solemnly lifted the Host. As all heads were bowed, the priest-assassin stabbed Giuliano in the back, and the rest of the Pazzi finished him off with eighteen more dagger blows. Lorenzo, who was armed, defended himself, and, with a wound to his neck, he escaped to the sacristy and bolted the door. Thinking that the Medici were dead, another conspirator, Archbishop Salviati, rushed to the Signoria, the government of the Republic of Florence, to demand their allegiance to the Pope. The Signoria consisted of nine citizens selected by drawing lots every two months. At the Palace of the Signoria, waiting to help Salviati, was a group of armed Pazzi supporters. But a mishap occurred. By mistake, they had locked themselves in the Chancery downstairs and couldn't get out! Shaken, Salviati headed upstairs, to face the Signoria, alone. Seeing him pale and stammering, the members of the Signoria, loyal to the Medici, seized him and hung him out of the window!

By now the city was in an uproar. The Pazzi were hung next to Archbishop Salviati – or beheaded. And nearly three hundred of their supporters were killed. Even mentioning the name 'Pazzi' was now forbidden by law in Florence.

Pope Sixtus excommunicated the Republic of Florence, and declared war. The Signoria, however, presented proof that the Pope had supported the conspiracy, and asked kings and princes of Europe for help. Most European monarchs sided with the Medici, but before anyone knew, Ferrante, the King of Naples, a friend of the Pope, invaded Tuscany and was marching on Florence.

'Death of Giuliano de' Medici' by Stefano Ussi

Lorenzo decided that instead of losing Florentine lives in the war, he would surrender himself to the King of Naples. The Signoria, however, refused to abandon him, and prohibited his sacrifice. But Lorenzo despised the Florentine government, his own puppets. In the middle of the night he slipped out of his palace, rode to Piza, sailed to Naples, and handed himself over to Ferrante. Ferrante was known for being an evil and treacherous ruler, but he was so stunned with Lorenzo's courage and patriotism, that he treated him as a guest of honor rather than as a prisoner. During the months of his stay in Naples, Lorenzo used his diplomatic genius to convince King Ferrante to abandon the Pope, and let him, Lorenzo, go home! And so, the reign of Lorenzo the Magnificent in Florence continued.

As Lorenzo tightened his grip on every aspect of life in Florence, he increased his government's spending on cultural projects. Huge amounts of money flowed to artists and architects, unheard-of salaries were paid to famous scholars who traveled from all over Italy to teach in Florence. Florence became the cultural capital of Italy and the first European city to fully embrace the Renaissance. Lorenzo supported a school of humanist philosophy – the Platonic Academy, which was part of his household. The best thinkers of Italy lived and taught ancient Greek philosophy, history, and literature at Lorenzo's palace. "My mind is aching from the noise of public affairs," wrote Lorenzo to a friend, "How could I survive without finding a refuge in learning?"

*"Lorenzo de' Medici's Platonic Academy" by Antonio Puccinelli*

*Lorenzo's Villa di Careggi – the meeting place of the Platonic Academy*

Lorenzo helped many famous artists of the Renaissance start their creative careers. He especially liked artists and scholars who openly flattered and praised him. Among his favorites were Filippino Lippi and Boticelli who often portrayed members of the Medici family in their paintings. Leonardo da Vinci also spent some time at the court of Lorenzo, but Lorenzo didn't like him as much, because Leonardo never said what he did not mean. One day Lorenzo saw a silver lute in the shape of a horse head that was built by Leonardo. He asked Leonardo to deliver it as a gift to the Duke of Milan. Leonardo used that opportunity to move to Milan and escape Lorenzo's circle of flatterers.

In the gardens of San Marco, Lorenzo had collected many Roman sculptures and works of art. This became the favorite place of teenage Michelangelo, who copied them to learn ancient sculpting techniques. Once Michelangelo copied a statue of a faun – the ancient Roman half-human, half-god mythological creature. Lorenzo instantly recognized that Michelangelo's version was far better than the ancient original. The faun's smile was much more real. Lorenzo teased the young artist saying, "This faun is old. Why does he have all his teeth? Old folks lose their teeth!" Michelangelo immediately took a hammer and knocked out several of the faun's teeth. Lorenzo laughed and invited Michelangelo to live in his palace with Lorenzo's sons.

Lorenzo spent more than half of the annual income of the Republic of Florence on books for the academy and university libraries. By 1490 the treasury of Florence was nearly empty. Lorenzo saved his own fortune by switching from banking to investing in real estate, but Florence was on the verge of bankruptcy. Under these darkening clouds, Lorenzo had to face a new enemy. A Dominican friar and priest, Savonarola, who was a passionate and talented preacher, grew immensely popular in Florence. He accused Lorenzo of corruption and raising taxes to hide his mismanagement of the city's finances. "The tyrant is distracting his citizens with spectacles and festivities, so that they ignore his evil schemes and leave the reins of power in his dirty hands!" raged Savonarola.

Lorenzo sent his friends to negotiate with Savonarola, but Savonarola demanded that Lorenzo be thrown out of Florence. To the shock of Lorenzo's friends, Savonarola also predicted that Lorenzo would die within a year. "He will go, and I will stay!" A year later, still in Florence, Lorenzo lay on his deathbed. His doctors couldn't diagnose his sickness. Pretending to treat him,

they ground precious pearls to powder, mixed that powder with water, and made Lorenzo drink it. That made Lorenzo even sicker. His days were numbered.

Of all the flatterers who surrounded him, Lorenzo trusted none. There was only one man in Florence who, he felt, had integrity. Lorenzo sent for Savonarola and asked him to absolve his sins. Savonarola refused unless Lorenzo fulfilled two conditions. The first was: "You must give up the wealth which you have taken by dishonest means." Lorenzo agreed to that without much hesitation. The second was: "You must restore political freedom in Florence." Lorenzo turned his face to the wall, thinking. Before he spoke again, he died. Two years after his death a revolt broke out, the Medici were driven into exile, and their palace was sacked by an angry mob.

Above: A portrait of Simonetta Vespucci by Boticelli. Simonetta Vespucci, a sister-in-law of Amerigo Vespucci, was the model in many of Boticelli's paintings. Right: Italian dagger, 1550

'Giuliano and Lorenzo de' Medici introduce Simonetta Vespucci to Sandro Boticelli' by Eleanor Fortescue-Brickdale.

# Leonardo da Vinci
## 1452–1519

On the sunny slopes of Monte Albano, a rocky hillside between Florence and Pisa, sat the little town of Vinci – an old castle and a few houses clinging to the castle walls. Here, in 1452, Leonardo, son of Ser Piero da Vinci, was born. His parents were not married when Leonardo was born, and soon his mother married another man. As a result Leonardo was raised by his father. Ser Piero was a successful lawyer who spent most of his time in Florence. When he was away Leonardo stayed with his grandmother, Mona Lena, who adored her talented grandson. Little Leonardo had blue eyes and wavy golden hair, but he liked to spend time alone in the woods and in the fields, and people of Vinci found that strange. When Leonardo was a baby, his mother had bought goat milk from a local woman who, many believed, was a witch. "What if her magic enchanted the boy?" they wondered. At seven Leonardo was sent to school, but he hated it and often skipped classes, hiding in the hills nearby. He was bored with Latin grammar. He felt he learned more by observing a spider weave its web, or by studying the structure of a flower. He also hated his schoolmates. Their games were rough, and when he saw them tearing wings off butterflies or beating a dog, he shook with anger. Mona Lena didn't tell Leonardo's father that his son was a disaster at school. But one time, when a complaint from the school reached Ser Piero da Vinci, Leonardo was locked in a closet for 3 days as punishment.

But soon things changed. When Leonardo started studying geometry, his progress was so rapid that his teachers were amazed. He convinced his father to buy him a lute and taught himself to play music. Neighbors started whispering again that the kid's talents had something to do with black magic. Soon Leonardo's family moved to Florence.

One day, Paolo dal Pozzo Toscanelli, a Florentine astronomer and mathematician, heard a knock on his door. He opened the door, and in walked 13-year-old Leonardo. "I would like to learn anything you can teach me," he said. When they started talking, Toscanelli realized that Leonardo's mind was capable of a depth of understanding that was rare even among scholars of that time. And Toscanelli knew a lot of scholars. He was a leader of the circle of scientists who searched for and studied mathematical works of ancient Greece. He was also famous for his inventions. In Florence cathedral you can still see his gnomon – an astronomical instrument that records the summer solstice to a half-second. Toscanelli taught Leonardo astronomy and math. Everyone thought Leonardo would become an astronomer, when, suddenly, Ser Piero came up with a better idea. He collected Leonardo's drawings scattered around the house and took them to the art studio of the famous Florentine painter Verrocchio. "Is this any good?" Ser Piero asked. Verrocchio who examined the drawings with deep interest. "Send your son to me at once," said Verrocchio. "He has, indeed, an amazing talent.'

Leonardo started studying art with Verrocchio, but Verrocchio was not happy with him. "Leonardo wants to know everything and do everything, and life is too short for that," he complained. Indeed, Leonardo never worked long on one project. He painted for a while, then switched to building mechanical toys, then he sculpted animals from clay, and then tried to construct some weird machine. "A waste of time," grumbled Verrocchio. "Do some real work and help me finish this picture of the Baptism for the good monks of Vallambrosa. Paint me an angel right here."

*'The Baptism of Christ' by Verrocchio and Leonardo*

Leonardo started painting, without thinking or making a sketch, as if the angel was in front of him and he was just painting his portrait. Verrocchio was speechless. Leonardo painted with amazing effortlessness, and his work was far superior to that of Verrocchio himself. Awe-struck, his students crowded behind him. Verrocchio turned to them. "Here is the real master," he said pointing at Leonardo. "And I will paint no more." They say that that day he quit painting!

*Gold florin of the Republic of Florence*

As everybody tried to get closer to the painting to see Leonardo's work, Leonardo quietly left the studio. He never seemed to notice any praise he received, and now he focused on something that had bothered him all day. On the way to the studio he had passed a tiny shop in a narrow street where they sold wild birds in cages. Leonardo felt sorry for the birds who were calling and beating their wings against the bars. He ran to the shop, and paid all the money he had to buy every single cage. One by one he opened the cages and let the birds out, as the townspeople stared at him in shock.

Even though Ser Piero always believed in his son, he was worried about Leonardo's future until one day a neighbor asked Leonardo to paint a monster on his shield. Leonardo went into the fields and caught all sorts of wild creatures – lizards, hedgehogs, newts, snakes, dragonflies, locusts, and bats. He brought them to his room, which no one was allowed to enter, and used them as models to paint a monster who was part lizard and part bat, with something of each of the other animals added to it. The monster came out so real that when Ser Piero opened the door to glance at the shield, he screamed and ran down the stairs! Once he realized it was just a painting, he sold it to a Florentine art dealer for 100 ducats. The dealer in turn sold it to the Duke of Milan, and Leonardo's neighbor was given a cheap shield bought on the local market.

Soon Leonardo started making good money doing art projects for Lorenzo the Magnificent, but he didn't like the atmosphere of flattery at Lorenzo's court and was happy to leave for Milan. Lorenzo sent him as a messenger to the Duke of Milan, but Leonardo was not planning to come back. Before leaving, he wrote a letter to the Duke of Milan describing all the things he could do both as an artist and engineer. He could design houses, create

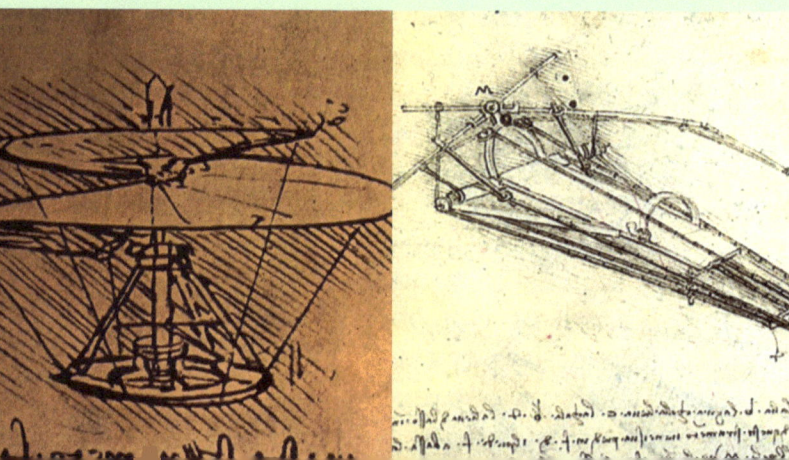

*'Lady with an Ermine' by Leonardo;
flying machines sketches by Leonardo:
on the left is the 'aerial screw' – a helicopter-type machine*

*'The Last Supper' by Leonardo da Vinci*

sculptures and paintings, build bridges, blow up castles, dig canals, invent a new kind of cannon, build warships, and make underground passages. The letter was written from right to left. This was how Leonardo always wrote, using his left hand, so that his letters could only be read by holding them next to a mirror. The Duke was amazed at the letter. "Either these are the words of a fool, or of a man of genius," he concluded and offered Leonardo a house and a salary.

Leonardo worked on many projects in Milan. One of the most famous is the mural of the Last Supper at the Dominican monastery of Santa Maria delle Grazie ("Holy Mary of Grace"). Leonardo worked on it for many years. Sometimes he didn't touch it for months, and sometimes he worked on it from morning till night, until suddenly he would put down his brushes and stand silently for a long time before the painting. Sometimes the Duke forgot to pay him, but Leonardo never seemed to even notice. He had a stable full of horses whom he loved like friends. His horses and his work made him happy.

But soon dark days fell on Milan. In 1500 King Louis XII of France attacked the city, captured the Duke of Milan and imprisoned him in a 6-foot-wide cage in a castle vault. Leonardo escaped to Venice and then to Florence. He worked as a military engineer for three years, creating a system of movable barricades to protect the city from attack. But then he started painting again. One of his new paintings was a portrait of Lisa del Giocondo, the wife of a Florentine silk merchant. As always Leonardo was on a quest for perfection. He ended up working on "Mona Lisa" for many years, almost until his death. In 1508 Leonardo returned to Milan. He lived in his old house and taught artists who came to study with him from all over Italy.

In 1513 Lorenzo Medici's son Giovanni became Pope Leo X and invited Leonardo to Rome where Leonardo lived for three years. Pope Leo gave Leonardo a salary and commissioned him a painting, but Leonardo was not interested in the Pope's projects. Instead, he started working on creating a new kind of varnish, experimented with quicksilver, practiced botany in the gardens of the Vatican, and studied anatomy by dissecting and examining dead bodies. The Pope was upset. He stopped giving Leonardo work.

The world of art was now worshipping other idols – the amazing Michelangelo and the young Raphael. It seemed as if it was Leonardo's fate to begin many things but to finish nothing. His great fresco "The Last Supper" was fading away, becoming dim and blurred. None of his sculptures survived. A few pictures remained, but these had never quite reached his ideal. His flying machine inventions – a wing-flapping ornithopter, an aerial screw (a helicopter-style rotor), and a parachute – were buried in his dusty notebooks. Many other inventions including hydraulic pumps, reversible crank mechanisms, gun shells with fins, and a steam cannon were never built and never even shown to anyone. Michelangelo had once scornfully told Leonardo he was a failure and couldn't

*'Mona Lisa'; below: 'Salvator Mundi' (Latin for 'Savior of the World') by Leonardo*

bring his projects to completion. So Leonardo started thinking of leaving Rome. Leonardo's hair was silver now, and his long beard was as white as snow.

In October 1515, King Francis I of France recaptured Milan and a year later Leonardo entered Francis' service. As a gift to the king, Leonardo created a mechanical lion. At a festive procession the lion walked forward several steps to meet the King, and then opened a door in its chest displaying a bouquet of lilies, the emblem of France. Leonardo lived in France until his death. King Francis often visited him, supported him financially, and became his close friend.

# SAVONAROLA
## 1452 – 1498

The Dominican monastery of San Marco in Florence faces a quiet square. Its walls are adorned with the frescoes of Fra Angelico. In one of his paintings St. Peter holds his finger to his lips asking for silence. In a monastic cell that once belonged to Savonarola you can see his desk where he wrote his sermons, and his portrait on the wall.

Girolamo Savonarola wanted to be a doctor, like his grandfather, but as a teenager he became interested in theology. At the age of nineteen, he fell in love with a girl whose parents would not allow her to marry him. His family, they said, was not as good as hers. This awakened Savonarola to the social inequalities around him, the oppression of the poor, and the vanity of the privileged. Around that time he wrote an essay entitled, *Contempt of the World*. Savonarola became a Dominican monk and was sent to live in Florence with the brothers of San Marco.

*Savonarola's cell; below: a Renaissance battle axe with the Medici coat of arms, 1500s*

Soon it became clear that the young Savonarola was a gifted preacher. At first his sermons seemed ordinary, but one day, as he spoke from the pulpit about Judgment Day, a sudden inspiration came upon him. He condemned the sins of men with such power that his audience wept and trembled. Some thought they saw a halo around his head. Savonarola kept preaching and suddenly he had a vision of a flaming sword, and heard voices promising the mercy of God to the faithful and the wrath of God to the unfaithful. He saw the sword lifted over Italy with lightning flashes and a crash of thunder. That vision moved Savonarola to use his talent against the puppet government of Florence and its master, Lorenzo the Magnificent. In his sermons he quoted the prophets of the Old Testament, and every prophet seemed to have something to say against Lorenzo.

Savonarola became so popular in Florence that he was elected the prior of the monastery of San Marco – even though he was an open enemy of Lorenzo, and Lorenzo was the greatest patron of the monastery. After the death of Lorenzo, a revolt broke out and the Medici family was thrown out of Florence. In the confusion that followed, Savonarola became the leader of a citizens' rebellion against the tyranny of the Medici. He drew up a new plan of government that put the public welfare above any private interests. Jesus Christ was solemnly proclaimed the king of Florence. The Florence cathedral could not hold the giant crowds that came to hear Savonarola preach about purifying the church and returning to the spirit of sacrifice the church had in its early days. Christ was speaking through him, insisted Savonarola. People of Florence started wearing modest clothes of dark colors, and, at celebrations, instead of songs filled with crude humor, they were now singing church hymns.

Meanwhile, the Medici turned for help to the King of France, Charles VIII. In 1494 Charles VIII invaded Italy and soon his army was at the gates of Florence. Savonarola saw this as a fulfillment of his prophetic vision: Charles was the sword of God raised to punish Florence for tolerating the criminal regime of the Medici. So at first he welcomed the invasion, but when Charles demanded that the Medici family come back to rule Florence, Savonarola began organizing resistance. Florentine citizens were building barricades, and throwing stones from windows at French soldiers.

*The Salone dei Cinquecento ('Hall of the Five Hundred') in the Palazzo Vecchio (the Palace of the Signoria in Florence), built in 1494 on commission of Savonarola*

'Savonarola Preaching Against Vanities' by Ludwig von Langenmantel

The Medici family had promised King Charles money and precious gifts if he returned Florence to their rule. Concerned that he would get nothing from the Medici, Charles demanded that the Signoria pay him to leave Florence. He showed up at the Palace of the Signoria and handed the leader of the Signoria, Piero Capponi, his ultimatum: Pay or suffer war and destruction. Capponi refused to pay. "Then we shall sound our trumpets," threatened the King. The trumpets would call his army to attack. "If you sound your trumpets, then we shall ring our bells!" said Capponi and tore up the king's ultimatum in Charles' face. The bells of the great cathedral of Florence would call the citizens to arm and fight. Florence was preparing for house-to-house combat. Unwilling to face an open rebellion, King Charles negotiated with the Signoria and left.

Savonarola was now even more popular than before. Florence was *the watchtower of Italy*, he said. From Florence the light of spiritual reform would shine on the whole of Italy and the rest of the Christian world. That idea did not amuse Pope Alexander VI. In 1495 the pope ordered Savonarola to come to Rome and explain himself. Savonarola sent the pope a list of excuses saying he was too sick to travel, he might be murdered on the road, and that it was not God's will for him to leave Florence. The Pope condemned Savonarola for pretending to be a prophet of God and forbade him to preach. The Pope belonged to the wealthy and corrupt Borgia family. Powerful families of Italy juggled positions of bishops, archbishops, cardinals, and popes, passing them to their family members as sources of easy income and political influence. Pope Alexander bribed with one hand and cursed with the other.

He also had a number of kids, even though, as a Catholic churchman, he was not supposed to either marry or have a family. In the eyes of Savonarola the name of Borgia was a synonym for shameless evil. Without hesitation Savonarola aimed his angry sermons at the pope.

He also continued to call the faithful to return to a simpler life and abandon their interest in luxury and love of humanist art and education. During the time of Carnival preceding Lent Savonarola began organizing his famous *bonfires of the vanities*. Every year citizens brought their *vanities* – thousands of items, such as fine clothes, jewelry, books, and paintings featuring stories from ancient Greek and Roman mythology – and burned them in a great bonfire on the city square, while the monks of San Marco danced around the flames. Mirrors, cosmetics, playing cards, precious fabrics, Roman sculptures, and musical instruments were piled on the Piazza della Signoria to be burned. Sandro Boticelli, one of Lorenzo Medici's favorite artists, deeply moved by the sermons of Savonarola, brought a few of his priceless paintings and hurled them into the flames. Other artists followed. Some scholars tossed into the fire their precious ancient Greek manuscripts from Byzantium. Gangs of Savonarola's supporters, called *the Weepers* (Piagnoni) roamed the city putting pressure on those who hesitated to part with their treasures.

And yet, with the immense power that was in the hands of Savonarola, his days were numbered. The city was growing tired of him. The humanist intellectuals of Florence, many of whom were from well-connected families of Europe, hated Savonarola for his fanaticism and hostility to arts and culture. There were also the monks of the Franciscan order, who were jealous of the popularity of the Dominicans. And there was the pope. Hoping to silence Savonarola with a bribe, Pope Alexander offered to make him a cardinal. But Savonarola rejected the offer. Then the Pope excommunicated Savonarola and ordered investigation of his teachings. Savonarola wrote a letter to the kings and princes of Europe asking them to summon a council to reform the Church and elect a new Pope. But it was too late.

*Pope Alexander with his son Cesare Borgia (left) and daughter Lucrezia – painting by John Collier*

The Franciscans proposed a trial by fire, according to a medieval custom. A Franciscan monk and a Dominican monk were to walk across the square between rows of blazing torches, and the one who got through safely would be proved to be right. Savonarola's right-hand man, Fra Domenico, foolishly accepted the challenge on behalf of the Dominicans. The rows of torches were built, and all Florence was there to see. But as the moment of trial arrived, both the Franciscans and the Dominicans hesitated. The crowd became restless. Fights broke out. Retreating to the monastery of San Marco, Savonarola and his friars were hooted and stoned. Next the monastery was stormed by a mob. The doors were broken down. Fra Domenico defended Savonarola with a huge candlestick, using it as a club. But Savonarola was arrested, and Domenico with him. They were put in chains and taken to the city square – Piazza della Signoria – where the Signoria's justice officer asked them if they still believed that Savonarola's teaching came from God. When they both replied 'yes,' they were thrown into jail and put on trial.

Cesare Borgia, a son of Pope Alexander VI and the head of the papal army, came to Florence to make certain Savonarola was tortured. Under torture Savonarola admitted that he did not receive prophecies from God, and that he had made everything up himself. The bishop who presided over the trial announced to him: "I separate you from the Church militant and from the Church triumphant." "Not from the Church triumphant," replied Savonarola. "That is beyond your power." Savonarola, Fra Dominico, and another monk were hanged, with the fire set under their feet. Even the bell of the church of San Marco that used to call the citizens to hear Savonarola's sermons was publicly exiled from the Dominican monastery and handed over to the Franciscans.

A bronze tablet in the pavement of the Piazza della Signoria shows where Savonarola was executed. Every year, on the anniversary of his death, a parade of citizens comes to the Piazza della Signoria to lay a wreath on that spot.

'Interrogation of Savonarola' by Francois Marius Granet

# Niccolo Machiavelli & Cesare Borgia
### 1469 – 1527          1475 – 1507

*Machiavelli*

Niccolo Machiavelli was a Florentine diplomat and writer. His name gave us the adjective *machiavellian* – sneaky, scheming and unscrupulous. It is often used to describe political strategies based on the principle *the end justifies the means* – reaching your goal by any means is justified, even if it takes lying, dirty deals, treachery, and outright crime. Yet Nicolo Machiavelli himself was an honest, highly-respected citizen of the Republic of Florence, a trusted secretary of the Signoria, and a diplomat. How did his name come to be associated with evil scheming? The reason is his book *The Prince*, where he created a portrait of a typical ruler of his time – successful because of his drive to power at any cost. Let us take a look at the events and historical personalities of Machiavelli's time that inspired him to write *The Prince*.

Born to a prominent Florentine family, Niccolo Machiavelli received an excellent education. He was familiar with humanist philosophy, read ancient Roman literature in Latin, and studied Ancient Greek authors in translation. In his 20s he saw the rebellion against the Medici, and the rise and fall of Savonarola. When Savonarola was forbidden to preach by the Pope, he went around the Papal order by preaching only to men at the monastery of San Marco. That's where young Machiavelli heard a couple of his sermons. Machiavelli could not understand what it was that attracted the citizens of Florence to Savonarola. In his eyes Savonarola was just an ignorant fanatic. "He is lashing at your books, your priests, and treating you in a way that even dogs would not tolerate... This friar is coloring his lies to suit the times!" wrote Machiavelli to a friend.

*Cesare Borgia*

Soon Machiavelli became a Secretary of the Signoria and started traveling on diplomatic missions. Observing the political scene around him, Machiavelli saw endless conspiracies, scandals, and invasions. Italy was divided into dozens of princedoms and republics. Bands of mercenaries roamed the land selling their swords to the highest bidder and dictating laws to friends and enemies alike. Sometimes when one republic was conquered by another, its citizens became mercenaries seeking in warfare the liberty they had lost at home. Of all the characters acting on the stage of history around him, Machiavelli was particularly fascinated with political adventurers – men who came from simple backgrounds, and rose to the heights of power commanding armies, heading rebellions, and becoming tyrants. The Medici came from rural Italy, the meaning of their name – 'doctors' – pointing to their humble origin. The Duke of Milan who employed Leonardo da Vinci, went from dirt to royalty in one generation: His father was a field laborer and began his military career as a stable boy. There were many such 'new princes' in Italy. The 15th century was rightly named the age of adventurers! Unlike Savonarola, whom Machiavelli viewed as an ultimate loser, calling him the 'weaponless prophet,' these new leaders were winners who each had some mysterious talent for success. What was that talent? That's the question Machiavelli sought to answer in *The Prince*.

*Frescoes by Domenico Ghirlandaio at Palazzo Veccio, Florence*

*Pope Alexander VI*

Of many tyrants and adventurers of his day one served as a major source of inspiration for Machiavelli's 'new prince' – Cesare Borgia, the son of Pope Alexander VI. As a churchman Pope Alexander VI was not supposed to have a family, but he did. He was also endlessly corrupt. His son Cesare was made a bishop at the age of 15, an archbishop at the age of 17, and a cardinal at the age of 18!! Show me a teenager who wants to be a cardinal! Cesare wanted to be a general. So at 19 he became the first cardinal ever to quit his position, and started a military career. He became the leader of a mercenary army serving the pope.

When Cesare showed up in Florence to ensure the conviction and execution of Savonarola, he was 23. His craving for power, ruthlessness, and greed were so extreme that most rulers of Italy shook in their shoes when he approached the walls of their cities. The Medici looked like innocent lambs next to Cesare Borgia. Machiavelli met him on his diplomatic missions and called him "a man without compassion, rebellious to Christ...the Hydra, the basilisk, deserving of the most wretched end." Yet it looked like there were lessons

*Savonarola rejects Pope Alexander's offer to be appointed cardinal – painting by Giulio Bargellini*

to be learned from Cesare Borgia's *modus operandi* (Latin for 'method or way of doing things'). In the years following the death of Savonarola, Pope Alexander, who adored Cesare, gave his son the task of bringing Central Italy under his control. Violence, treason, and endless bloodshed were ordinary tools in the hands of the Borgia. But the Borgia were also patrons of the arts, and Cesare hired Leonardo da Vinci as a military engineer.

Machiavelli concluded that for a ruler it was better to be feared than to be loved. A ruler could not be bound by loyalties, traditions, or ethics. The key to the success of the Borgia was a total absence of any moral code. They built their state and their reputation by brutal force, deceit, and division, rather than by diplomacy and winning people to their side. That's the only way to hold to power, advised Machiavelli in *The Prince*.
*Divide et impera!* – 'Divide and rule' in Latin.

On his diplomatic missions to Rome, Machiavelli observed first-hand how the Borgia operated. Cesare's mercenaries had to be paid, and on time. He was spending over 1000 ducats a day. Some money came from robbery and pillage, and more was sent to Cesare by the pope.
To raise the money for his son's conquests, and to pay his own gambling debts, Alexander VI was selling the positions of bishops and cardinals. Eighty new bishops' offices sold at 750 ducats apiece. Nine men with criminal records were made cardinals upon payment of more than 20,000 ducats each. But that was not enough. The pope also poisoned his own friends and pillaged their houses. Cardinal Orsini, who had been close to the pope, suddenly fell sick and was immediately arrested and thrown in jail. His family suspected he was poisoned on the order of the pope. His mother offered the Pope 25,000 ducats as a ransom. The pope rejected the money. Then she sent him a large pearl he had always wanted to have. He accepted the pearl but did not grant Orsini the pardon. Soon Orsini was dead. His family was driven out of their house, and allowed to take with them only the clothes they wore. The house was pillaged and sold for gold.

Whoever had money in Rome trembled for their lives. Even the Medici who found refuge at the papal court were terror-stricken. The pope passed his time gambling, attending horse races, and enjoying public festivals and celebrations, but the situation in Rome was getting tense. The pope asked Cesare Borgia to come and support him in Rome. Cesare turned toward Rome, spreading devastation on his way. When he drew near the town of San Quirico, all the inhabitants had fled except a few old people. Cesare hung them by their arms, with a slow fire under their feet, to make them reveal where the town treasury was hidden. They were clueless, so they had to die. Cesare committed similar atrocities in every town on his way.

Finally he entered Rome with a few cardinals and servants – all wearing leather masks. Everybody recognized Cesare, but he kept his mask on. The fear of faceless terror spread all over the city.

A few days later another cardinal died in the middle of the night after two days of violent sickness. Before dawn his house was searched and more than 150,000 ducats in gold and precious stones were brought to the pope. Again, there were rumors of poisoning. The Venetian ambassador complained he could not be received because everybody at the pope's court was busy counting the money. The next day the pope called him and showed him a pile of gold. "See, there are only 23,832 ducats," said the pope, "yet the rumor is I got over 100 thousand ducats in gold!" He expected us to support his lie, reported the Venetian ambassador. More arrests followed. Random wealthy people were accused of being heretics and thrown in jail. Cesare's men broke into their houses, stripping them of all their contents. Then Cesare made deals with the families of the 'heretics' to release them for large sums of money.

"Cesare Borgia leaving the Vatican with the treasures of Pope Alexander VI" by Giuseppe-Lorenzo Gatteri; left: "A kiss" – Italian Renaissance dish, 1520–1550

And then, in 1503, something unexpected happened. The pope himself fell sick. And so did Cesare. Now the rumor was, the pope and Cesare had been planning to poison Cardinal Adriano, but the cup-bearer had made a mistake, and given the poisoned wine to the Borgia. Yet another rumor said that Cardinal Adriano had figured out he was the next to be poisoned and had paid the cup-bearer a bribe of 10,000 ducats to poison the Borgia instead! Cesare's right-hand man Don Michele broke into the pope's apartments, and closing the doors, held a dagger to the throat of the cardinal who was in charge of the pope's household, threatening to kill him and throw him out of the window if he did not immediately give Don Michele the pope's keys and money. The cardinal gave him the keys. More than 300,000 ducats in gold, silver and jewels were taken to Cesare. At last the death of the pope was announced. The pope's dead body got terribly swollen and turned black, confirming death by poisoning. Pope Alexander VI was so hated in Rome that the workmen were joking and insulting the pope's memory while digging his grave. The carpenters, having made the coffin too short, pulled off the pope's mitre, and stuffed his body into the coffin.

A new pope was elected, but he was sick too, and died 26 days later. Then, the Borgia's deadly enemy, Giuliano Della Rovere, was elected Pope Julius II. This marked the end of the political career of Cesare Borgia. He was only 28 years old. Cesare begged the new pope for forgiveness and mercy. He blamed his youth, his bad advisors, and his evil father. He promised to give back all the property he had stolen from the pope's apartment. Machiavelli was shocked. Now he felt nothing but contempt for his favorite 'prince.' Cesare fled Rome but was soon captured and locked up in a castle in Spain. He escaped but was captured again, and yet again he escaped. After a final betrayal by his mercenaries Cesare was wounded in combat and left dying on a battlefield, robbed and naked. Even his favorite leather mask was gone.

Like the Borgia family, Florence also relied on mercenary troops. Machiavelli decided to change that. Mercenaries could not be trusted. He started training and arming the citizens of Florence to form the Florence militia. Meanwhile, the Medici went the familiar route. In 1512 they hired Spanish mercenaries, defeated the Florence militia, abolished the Florentine Republic, and banished Machiavelli from the city. A year later they accused him of conspiracy and threw him in jail. After three weeks of torture Machiavelli still denied he was guilty. So the Medici released him and let him live on his farm. From then on Machiavelli wrote his books, traveled, and corresponded with prominent politicians of his day. The Latin inscription on his tomb reads: *Tanto nomini nullum par elogium.* – To such a name no praise is enough.

# MICHELANGELO
## 1475 – 1564

Michelangelo was born in the town of Caprese (today called Caprese Michelangelo) to Lodovico Buonarroti. Lodovico was the *podesta* – the mayor of the town. Because Michelangelo was born on a Sunday, the wise men of the town declared his birth to be a sign from heaven, so Lodovico called his baby boy *Michael Angelo*, after the archangel Michael. Michelangelo's mother died when he was six. The boy was sent to live with his nanny and her husband, a stonecutter who worked at a marble quarry. Years later Michelangelo said that breathing the pure mountain air and watching stone cutting were some of his earliest memories.

Lodovico wanted his son to go into business and make money for the family, but Michelangelo wanted to be an artist and spent every spare moment making sketches on the walls of his father's house. Lodovico didn't want to hear about art. He beat his son to make him quit his silly ideas, but Michelangelo wouldn't give up.

This was at the time when Florence had become the greatest European center of the arts, with the Signoria, the artists' guilds, and wealthy patrons all ready to pay huge sums of money to talented sculptors and painters. So Lodovico sent his stubborn 13-year-old son to study with the famous Florentine master Ghirlandaio who had the biggest art studio in Florence. Ghirlandaio's new student made such rapid progress that a year later he was paid like a professional artist – unheard of for a kid of 14! But then Michelangelo started correcting the drawings of his teacher. The boy also had a habit of saying exactly what he thought. Ghirlandaio was not amused, and when Michelangelo was 16 he had to leave Ghirlandaio's studio. Michaelangelo never had another art teacher. Fortunately, Ghirlandaio had enough appreciation for Michaelangelo to recommend him to Lorenzo the Magnificent. To the great astonishment of Lodovico Buonarotti, his son was invited to live at the Medici palace and was treated as a celebrity.

Together with other young artists, Michelangelo would often go to study frescoes by Masaccio in the chapel of the Carmine. Young artists working there began to look with envious feelings at Michelangelo's drawings, and their jealousy grew as his fame increased. One day, a youth called Pietro Torrigiano made some scornful remarks about Michelangelo's work. When Michelangelo ignored him, Pietro smashed Michelangelo's face with a fist and broke his nose.

When Lorenzo the Magnificent died, Michelangelo continued to live at the court of Lorenzo's son Piero, but Piero wasn't excited about marble sculptures. He asked Michelangelo to make him a statue of snow! Imagine a snowman by Michelangelo!

When the revolt against the Medici broke out and Savonarola took over the city, his preaching appealed to Michelangelo's sense of justice and deeply moved him. It is believed that Savonarola's sermons inspired Michelangelo's fresco 'The Last Judgement' which he painted many years later on the altar wall of the Sistine Chapel in the Vatican. But Savonarola was hostile to art and artists, so Michelangelo followed the Medici into exile. He was next employed by Lorenzo di Pierfrancesco de' Medici, a relative of Lorenzo the Magnificent, who grew up at his court, wrote poetry and was a patron of the arts. He was also a friend and an employer of Amerigo Vespucci. It was to Lorenzo di Pierfrancesco that Amerigo wrote his famous letters describing the newly-discovered continent.

Once, to Michelangelo's surprise, Lorenzo asked him to create a statue that looked like it had been buried under some ruins for centuries. He wanted to sell it to a collector of ancient art in Rome. Michelangelo agreed. The collector who purchased his work, Cardinal Riario, quickly figured out the sculpture was a fake, but he was so impressed with its quality that he found out who was its real sculptor and invited Michelangelo to Rome.

*Drawings by Michelangelo*

When Michelangelo arrived in Rome he was 21. In Rome he received a commission to sculpt the 'Pieta' – Mary weeping over the body of the crucified Jesus. When Michelangelo completed the 'Pieta' three years later, the art world instantly recognized it as a true masterpiece. Michelangelo never signed his art works, but one day he overheard someone admiring 'Pieta.' Because there was no signature, the visitors thought the sculpture was created by another artist. So, after dark, when all the art lovers had left, Michelangelo came back to the statue and carved his name on it. This is why the Pieta is the only sculpture that bears Michaelangelo's signature.

Michelangelo's sculptural works look so full of life that many people described his work as breathing life into marble. In Michelangelo's own words, "I saw the angel in the marble and carved until I set him free." Soon Michelangelo became so famous that in artistic circles they started calling him *Il Divino* – 'the divine one.'

Even though he always complained that his employers were not paying him enough and not paying on time, Michelangelo was able to buy four farms and other properties as well! Patrons of arts felt it was an honor to send a gift of cash to the famous artist, so Michelangelo's fortune grew and grew. One of the cardinals from the Medici family once heard that Michelangelo liked his beautiful Arabian horse. He sent it right away to Michelangelo as a gift. Michelangelo's biographer Giorgio Vasari wrote in *Lives of the Most Excellent Painters, Sculptors, and Architects*: "Although he was rich, he lived like a poor man... This sober life kept him very active. He needed very little sleep, and often during the night he would rise to work on his sculptures. Having made himself a cap of thick paper, he fixed a lighted candle in the middle of the cap. This way his hands were free and the candle threw light over where he was working."

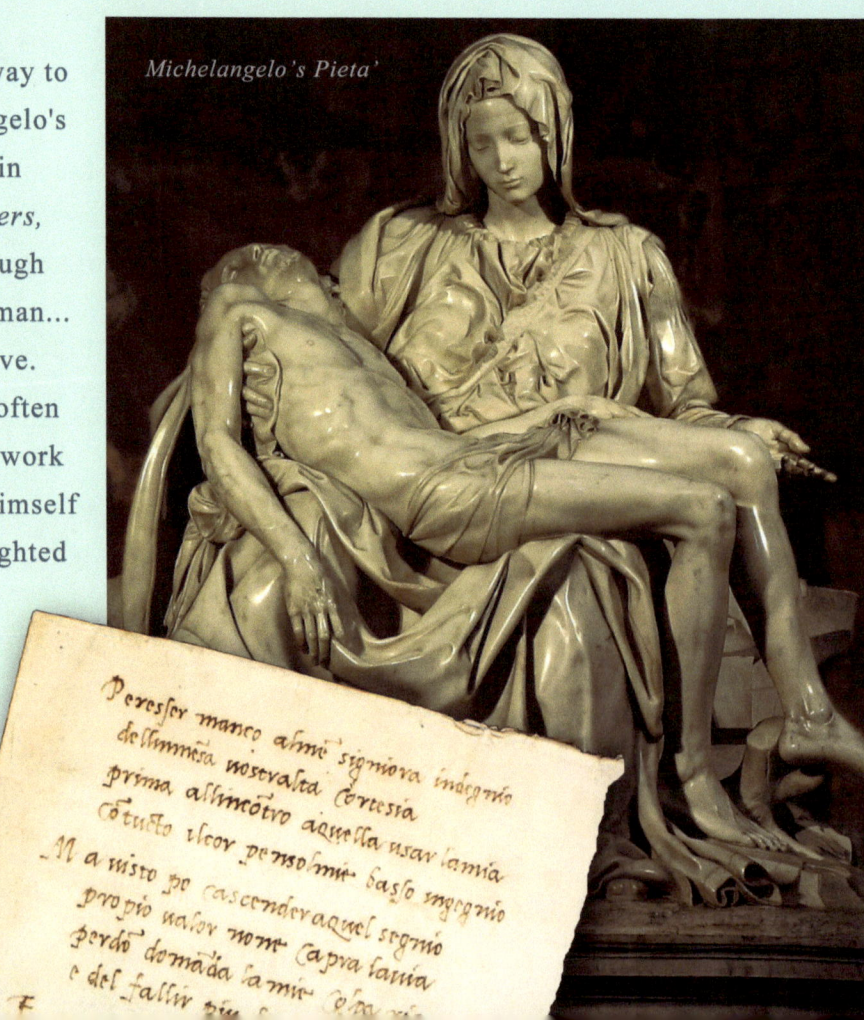

*Michelangelo's Pieta'*

*Michelangelo's hand-written sonnet to Vittoria Colonna*

In 1505 Pope Julius II commissioned Michelangelo to build the pope's tomb. He asked Michelangelo to make forty statues and finish the project in 5 years. The most famous among the statues Michelangelo completed for the tomb is that of Moses. But some artists were feeling envious about Michelangelo's success. One of them was Donato Bramante, an architect who was working on rebuilding St. Peter's Basilica. Bramante convinced the pope that it was an evil omen to build his own tomb. Also, knowing that Michelangelo was mostly a sculptor and not a painter, he suggested to the pope that instead of carving sculptures for the tomb Michelangelo should paint the ceiling of the Sistine Chapel.

When the pope ordered Michelangelo to start the Sistine Chapel project, Michelangelo refused, saying he was not good at the art of painting. "Didn't they teach you to mix colors in the studio of Ghirlandaio?" asked Pope Julius, annoyed. Michelangelo had never painted frescoes before. He asked a couple painters to show him some basic technique, but then kicked them out.

*Tomb of Pope Julius II; Moses by Michalangelo*

To paint the ceiling he had to lie flat on a scaffolding for hours, but he accepted no help. One day he fell off the scaffolding and was hurt. He had to stay in bed for weeks. The final composition of the Sistine Chapel ceiling covered 500 square meters and included 300 figures. Pope Julius was very anxious for Michelangelo to complete the project. "When will you finish it?" he kept asking every day. "When I can," grumbled Michelangelo. One day the pope got so angry about this that he hit Michelangelo with his staff, but then, scared that Michelangelo would quit, sent him a gift of 500 ducats.

Seeing that Michelangelo was incredibly successful as a painter, Donato Bramante tried to convince the pope to take the Sistine Chapel project away from Michelangelo and give it to Raphael! That was one of the reasons Michelangelo couldn't stand Raphael. "All he achieved in art, he got from me," he complained. Once he ran into Raphael in the street. He was alone, while Raphael was accompanied by a group of friends. "Only a chief of police walks around with a troop like this," Michelangelo observed. "Only an executioner walks alone," replied Raphael.

Decades later Michelangelo painted another masterpiece in the Sistine Chapel – The Last Judgment, covering the entire altar wall. Michelangelo worked on The Last Judgement for seven years. When the fresco was almost finished, Biagio da Cesena, the master of ceremonies of Pope Paul III, saw his work and complained to the pope that Michelangelo was portraying saints and characters from the Bible almost naked, in the style of ancient Greek and Roman sculptures. When The Last Judgment was finally unveiled, everyone saw Biagio, almost naked and with donkey ears, painted as one of the devils in hell! Biagio ran complaining to the pope. "God has given me authority in heaven and on earth," Paul III told him, "but my authority does not extend into hell. I cannot free you from there."

In 1546, Michelangelo was appointed an architect of St. Peter's Basilica – an ancient church built by Constantine the Great, the first Christian Emperor of Rome, in the 4th century, on the burial place of St. Peter. Before Michelangelo a few architects worked on the plans for the new cathedral, including Bramante and Raphael. Michelangelo finalized the building plans and designed the grand dome of St. Peter's Basilica – still one of the tallest domes in the world.

Not only was Michelangelo a great artist, he was also a spectacular poet, who left over 300 poems. He was a devout Christian – many of his poems express the depth and loyalty of his faith. Michelangelo never had a family. Late in life he fell in love with a noblewoman, a widow, and a poetess, Vittoria Colonna. He was 61 and she was 46. Vittoria was deeply religious and after the death of her husband she wanted to become a nun, but her brother convinced the pope to refuse her wish. Her family hoped she would marry again and bring them more power and connections through a new marriage. Many noblemen proposed to her, but she rejected them all, and lived alone writing poetry. Loyalty to the memory of her husband prevented Vittoria from seeking romantic relationships, but she remained a friend of Michelangelo. They wrote poems to each other. Vittoria also wrote a whole book of Christian poetry for Michelangelo. Here is a translation of a sonnet Michelangelo wrote for Vittoria Colonna:

*Vittoria Colonna, a sketch by Michelangelo*

*A portrait of Vittoria Colonna, by Sebastiano del Piombo; below left: a jug produced at the Medici porcelain workshop, 1575 – 1587*

*How can it be, Lady, as we can see
from long experience, that an image
sculpted in hard marble lasts longer than its maker,
whom the years turn to ashes?
The cause bows down to the effect,
from which it's clear that art defeats nature.
And I know, for I prove it true in beautiful sculpture,
that time and death can't destroy my work.
Therefore, I can give both of us
endless life in colors or stone,
by depicting our faces, so that
a thousand years after we are gone
people will see how lovely you were,
and how wretched I was,
and how, in loving you,
I was no fool.*

Ten years after they met, Vittoria died and with her death all brightness for Michelangelo faded. Michelangelo lived to be a very old man, but his life was lonely and solitary to the end.

# RAPHAEL
## 1483 – 1520

Raphael inherited his love of art from his father who was a court painter to the Duke of Urbino. Raised at the court, Raphael grew up with elegant manners and sophisticated taste. He moved easily between artistic and aristocratic circles. When Raphael was 8, his father sent him to study with the great Renaissance artist Pietro Perugino. "He is my pupil now, but soon he will be my master," Perugino used to say as he watched Raphael at work.

At age 25, already famous and nicknamed 'the Prince of painters,' Raphael moved to Rome at the invitation of Pope Julius II. He lived there for 12 years, until his death, working at the Vatican. Raphael had a workshop of fifty students. Some of his frescoes on the walls of the Vatican palace were actually painted by his students who copied Raphael's drawings and finished them on their own.

In his book "Lives of the Most Excellent Painters, Sculptors, and Architects" Giorgio Vasari says that Bramante, who had a set of the keys to the Sistine Chapel, secretly led Raphael to take a peek at the unfinished work of Michelangelo – the frescoes on the ceiling of the chapel. Even though Michelangelo and Raphael hated each other, Michelangelo clearly influenced Raphael's style. In his "School of Athens" fresco, Raphael painted a portrait of Michelangelo as the ancient Greek philosopher Heraclitus. This may have been a tribute of respect. Heraclitus was famous for his philosophy of universal change: The world is always evolving, nothing stays the same. "When you step into the same river, the water that flows in it is always new," he said. But it's also possible that Michelangelo's portrait as Heraclitus was a hint at Michelangelo's unfriendly attitude. Heraclitus was known for his misanthropy. *Misanthropy* means 'hatred of men', from the Greek *misos* – hatred, and *anthropos* – man. Heraclitus had nothing but scorn for the famous philosopher and mathematician Pythagoras, and thought that Homer should have been beaten for his 'useless' poems.

Raphael's art made him wealthy and independent. Just like Leonardo and Michelangelo, he hardly cared about the opinions of critics or powerful patrons about his art. Once two cardinals watched him work on a fresco featuring the apostles Peter and Paul. The cardinals complained that the face of the apostle Paul was too red, as if he blushed. Irritated, Raphael responded: "He blushes to see into whose hands the church has fallen."

Most of us associate Raphael's work with the iconic style of Renaissance painting.
How did the Renaissance style differ from the art of the Middle Ages?
Let's place side-by-side two paintings depicting the same story: Christ carrying the cross.
The first painting is by the Italian painter Simone Martini. It is in the Gothic style – the style of the early 14th century. The second painting (next page) is by Raphael.

The main differences between the medieval and Renaissance styles of painting are the use of perspective, the use of light, and correct proportions. Perspective is a drawing technique that creates the illusion of depth, where objects far away are smaller, and objects closer to the viewer are bigger. Raphael's figures are anatomically correct, and his landscape is 3-dimensional and realistic. Simone Martini's painting is flat, with no perspective and no 'space' between figures: Everyone looks all 'glued' together. In Simone Martini's painting the city buildings in the background are too small next to the figures of the people who are coming out of the city gate. And those people look bigger than the figures that are much closer to us. The interplay of light and shade in Raphael's painting creates a dynamic composition that draws your eye to the figures of Christ and Mary. In Simone Martini's work only the red color of Christ's robe brings your attention to his figure.

Otherwise the composition is messy and unfocused. Also, notice how realistically Raphael portrays emotions. The gestures and the expressions of his characters' faces are both dramatic and credible. Simone Martini's characters look like mediocre actors on stage. Gothic style paintings used a lot of gold and a lot of detail in depicting clothes and architecture. All this disappeared in Renaissance art. To create that strong 3-dimensional feeling, Raphael works like a sculptor playing with light and shade. He avoids small details that can take the focus away from the poses, gestures, and facial expressions of his characters.

# MARTIN LUTHER
## 1483 – 1546

In 1517 a German monk nailed a sheet of paper to the door of All Saints' Church in Wittenberg. The paper contained a series of 95 theses written in Latin, and addressed to theologians. *Theses* is plural of the Greek word *thesis* – proposition, statement. The writer was wondering about the church practice of selling indulgences: Was it in accordance with God's truth as stated in the Bible?

When Pope Leo X wanted to raise money for the rebuilding of St. Peter's Basilica in Rome, he did it by the sale of indulgences. The word *indulgence* comes from the Latin *indulgentia* – a pardon. In the early years of Christianity an indulgence was a pardon of sins granted by the church in exchange for a penance, such as charity work, saying prayers, or going on a pilgrimage to visit holy places. However in the course of the Middle Ages corrupt churchmen started selling indulgences for cash. In 1516 Pope Leo sent Dominican friar Johann Tetzel to sell indulgences in Germany.

Tetzel held huge meetings in town squares. He started by preaching about sins and hell, and ended by selling stacks of indulgences. "All sins may be forgiven!" thundered Tetzel. "Here is the promise of the pope, here are letters of indulgence, here is the opportunity for a little money to save your soul! And what about your dead parents? What if they are in hell? You can save them too! Can you hear your dead parents crying out, 'Have mercy upon us? We are burning here in hell and you can set us free for very little money?'"

*The door of All Saints' Church, Wittenberg, with Luther's Theses engraved on it.*
*Photo by A. Savin*

Tetzel also used to say: "As soon as the coin in the coffer rings, the soul into heaven springs!"

The monk who posted the paper about indulgences on the church door in Wittenberg was Martin Luther. Luther believed that forgiveness was God's alone to grant, and that the sale of indulgences was a corrupt practice invented by church leaders for self-enrichment. Like many thinkers of his day, Martin Luther was awakened by the spirit of independence that was everywhere in the era of the Renaissance. The growing use of firearms and the invention of the printing press were changing society. A common man with a gun could defeat a knight on horseback, and a common man with a book was able to question scholarly teachings and the doctrines of the church. We tend to associate Martin Luther's name with the Reformation rather than the Renaissance, but remember: He was born in the same year as Raphael – 1483.

Luther was born into a family of a copper miner. He made his way through school on his own, and at 17 entered the University of Erfurt to study law. He also studied humanist philosophy, but its focus on reason was unsatisfying to Luther. One day, as he was riding a horse on his way home, lightning struck only a few steps away from him. Terrified he cried, "Help! Saint Anna! If I survive, I will become a monk!" St. Anna was the patron saint of miners. The fear he experienced had such an impact on Luther that he sold his books, left the university, and joined St. Augustine's Monastery.

At the monastery he was tortured by feelings of guilt and doubt. He went through years of deep depression, fasting and praying. For days he didn't eat or drink, consumed by a fear of hell. "I lost touch with Christ the Savior and Comforter, and made him the jailer and hangman of my poor soul," he said later describing that period of his life. One of his fellow monks advised him: "Martin, you are a fool. God is not angry with you; it is you who are angry with God." The head of the monastery and Luther's confessor, Johann von Staupitz, tried to set Luther at ease: "You have no real sin, Martin," he told the young monk. "You make a sin out of every little thing." Staupitz guessed that what Luther really needed was not focusing on his own sins, but ministering to other people.

In 1507 Luther was ordained a priest, and the following year, when Staupitz became dean of the theological faculty at the University of Wittenberg, he hired Luther as a professor of logic and ethics. Martin Luther also started studying Hebrew and Greek – the original languages of the Bible. The official version of the Bible was the Latin *Vulgata*. Nobody in Europe read the Bible in their native language – German, English, French... The educated read it in Latin, and the common people heard bible stories only in sermons, or saw them depicted on church walls. But the spirit of the Renaissance was sweeping Europe: More and more scholars, including Luther, considered translating the Bible into local languages.

Soon Luther became the most popular preacher in town, and the most popular professor at the university. He started coming up with new ways to interpret church doctrine. For example, he criticized the common way of thinking about the saints. Instead of trying to be like them, people were praying to the saints seeking their help. "We call on the saints," said Luther, "only when we feel pain, or when our pockets are empty." People listened, ready for change.

Luther's Ninety-Five Theses were translated from Latin into German and spread around Europe like wildfire. Pope Leo X was used to attacks by heretics. When he heard of the Ninety-Five Theses, he said: "A drunken German wrote that. When he is sober, he will think differently." But soon he changed his tune and summoned Luther to Rome to be put on trial. Luther refused to go. He was offered a position of a bishop on the condition that he stops speaking up against the Catholic Church. Luther rejected the offer. Instead he started questioning the authority of the pope. Was he indeed the representative of Christ on earth? Was his every word the truth, and his will the law?

*"Martin Luther and the university professors burning the pope's bull" by Karl Aspelin*

Luther declared that only the Bible was the source of authority in all matters of faith and church life. He rejected those portions of the church tradition that did not come from the Bible, such as revelations received by saints, and practices like selling indulgences. This doctrine became known as *sola scriptura* – Latin for 'by scripture alone.'

Another question that split the Protestant movement from the Catholic Church was: How can a sinner be saved? The church taught the doctrine of salvation by grace. Grace is a blessing given by God through the Church. People receive it in church through the sacraments. Luther agreed that salvation is by grace, but he taught that grace is given to anyone who has faith. And since faith is between the individual and God, there is no need for priests, sacraments, or even the Catholic church. Even righteous deeds, such as acts of kindness and charity, are gifts of God's grace, taught Luther, not something that comes from people's free will. This doctrine became known as the 'justification by faith alone' – *justificatio sola fide* in Latin, or simply *sola fide* – 'by faith alone.'

In 1520, the pope excommunicated Luther. Excommunication is the exclusion of a person from taking communion and participating in other sacraments of the church. But Luther had so much support that the professors and students of the university burned the pope's bull – his order. Martin Luther was permitted to explain himself before a council representing German cities and states. The English term for that assembly is *diet* from Latin *dieta* – parliamentary assembly. The council met in the city of Worms, which – in English – gave it the funny name of the *Diet of Worms*. Luther defended himself before the council with a pile of his own books on the table. Asked if he stood by all that he had written in those books, he answered that he would change his mind only if he could be proved wrong based on what is actually written in the Bible.

*"Luther at the Diet of Worms" by Anton von Werner*

The result was a condemnation. Luther's books were to be burned, he was declared an outlaw, and was to be imprisoned. Nobody could offer him food or shelter, and anyone could kill him without consequences. Before the final decision was published, Luther left Worms. But on the road to Wittenberg, in a forest, a company of armed masked horsemen stopped Luther. Pretending they were robbers, they scared away Luther's companions, and took him by secret paths through the woods to the castle of Wartburg. There he found himself among friends. The kidnapping was arranged by Frederick the Wise, a German prince who supported Luther and wanted him to sit out the storm in a safe hiding place. Martin Luther lived in Wartburg for nearly a year, while all the world wondered what had become of him. It was clear he was still alive, because he continued to write and publish letters promoting his views. When the Archbishop of Mayence tried to resume selling indulgences, he quickly received a letter from Luther and promptly changed his plans.

During that year Luther completed his translation of the New Testament from Greek into German. Later, with the help of other scholars, he translated the Old Testament, finishing his full Bible translation in 1534. Meanwhile the Reformation became a movement that spread across Europe. Now the Protestants were also dividing among themselves. Some were moderate and others were radical. And all together they opposed the Renaissance humanist scholars led by Dutch Christian philosopher Erasmus of Rotterdam. Erasmus pursued truth on the basis of reason and free will, following the tradition of ancient Greece and Rome. Luther, however, denied freedom of will. He replaced the authority of the Church with the authority of the Bible. His idea was that men were not to reason about religion, but to take it just as they found it in the Scriptures. That's where Martin Luther lost the support of Renaissance scholars. Meanwhile the peasants' uprising known as the Peasants' War, was sweeping over Germany.

"Luther's family" by Gustav Spengenberg

Mobs of impoverished and desperate men armed with clubs and torches burned towns and monasteries, and killed landowners and priests. Luther's enemies declared that this was the natural consequence of Luther's teaching. Luther disagreed. He denounced the peasants, and urged the princes to 'shoot them like mad dogs.' Many rebels were discouraged by this condemnation and the uprising was suppressed.

In April 1523 a noblewoman and a nun, 24-year-old Katharina von Bora, who lived in a Cistercian convent, contacted Martin Luther asking for help. She had become interested in the ideas of Reformation and conspired with a few other nuns to escape from the convent. Luther sent to the convent a merchant who usually delivered herring for the nuns. The merchant arrived with a wagon and empty herring barrels, hid twelve nuns in the barrels, and safely transported them out of the monastery. Two years later Martin Luther married Katharina von Bora. Luther's friends tried to talk him out of the marriage. Because he had been ordained a priest, breaking his priestly vows would destroy his reputation, they said. But Luther decided that his marriage "would please his father, annoy the pope, make angels laugh, and devils weep." Among witnesses at the wedding was Lucas Cranach the Elder, a German painter famous for the portraits of many prominent figures of the German Renaissance, including Luther. Martin and Katharina had six children. Katharina managed Luther's household and a dormitory for his students, ran a brewery, a cattle farm, and a hospital where she worked as a nurse.

*Above: A portrait of Katharina von Bora by Lucas Cranach the Elder; below: "Wittenberg, October 31, 1517" by Eyre Crowe; right: German Renaissance pendant with the Holy Family and Crucifixion*

# KING HENRY VIII & ST. THOMAS MORE
## 1491 – 1547              1478 – 1535

Henry VIII became the King of England in 1509, when he was 17. Having received a Renaissance-style education, he was familiar with humanist philosophy, science, and the classical literature of ancient Greece and Rome. He wrote books and composed music. Early in his reign he was loyal to the Catholic Church. He even published a book *Assertio Septem Sacramentorum* (Latin for 'Defence of the Seven Sacraments') condemning ideas of Martin Luther, for which Pope Leo X gave him the title *Fidei Defensor* – Latin for 'Defender of the Faith.'

Soon after his coronation, Henry VIII married Catherine of Aragon, the widow of his older brother, but after a while he decided to divorce her. All their children had died in infancy except for one, a girl, the future Queen Mary. The King believed a woman could not inherit the English throne. Also he fell in love with a young noblewoman of the court, the gorgeous and spectacularly-educated Anne Boleyn. In 1527 Henry VIII asked the pope to annul (declare invalid) his marriage to Catherine. But the pope refused. He didn't want to upset Catherine of Aragon's powerful family. So the king convinced the Archbishop of Canterbury to declare his marriage 'null and void,' and married Anne Boleyn in a secret wedding ceremony. Queen Catherine was kicked out of the palace. Her rooms now belonged to Anne. Anne was confident, and behaved like a queen, receiving foreign diplomats and advising the king.

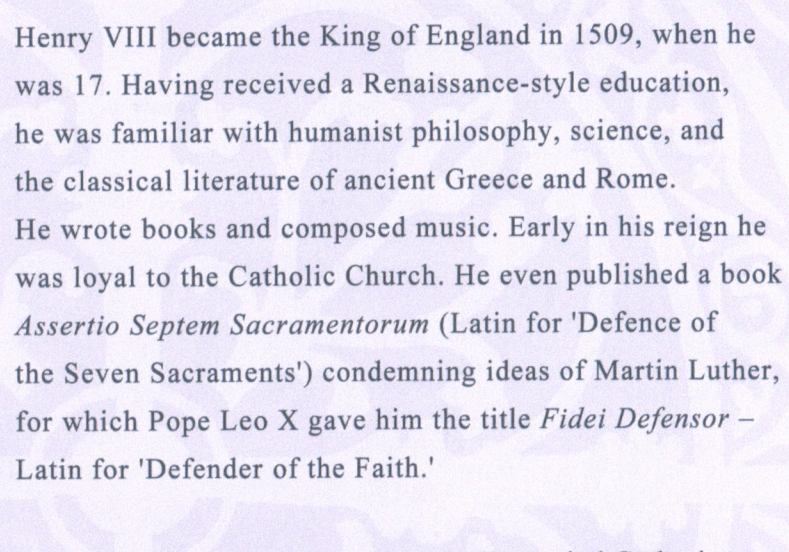

*Renaissance signet ring with initials R.S., late 15th century*

Henry VIII was so angry at the pope that he broke all connections with Rome and the Catholic Church. The pope's authority in England was abolished. By act of Parliament Henry was declared "Supreme head of the Church of England." So unlike the Protestant movement in Germany and Switzerland, the English Reformation began with the rulers, not the people, and was political rather than religious in nature.

English translations of the Bible played an important role in breaking further away from the Catholic Church. The first was done more than 100 years before King Henry VIII, by Oxford University scholar John Wycliffe. For this Wycliffe was proclaimed a heretic. Possession of Wycliffe bibles was punished by death. The next English translation of the Bible was done by William Tyndale in the 1520s. After years in hiding, Tyndale was captured by Catholic authorities in Antwerp and executed as a heretic. However, after Henry VIII broke with the pope, printed copies of English-language bibles were placed in churches. They had to be chained to the reading desks so nobody could take them home.

Everyone wanted to have a copy! Often so many people wanted to read the English bible at once that it had to be read aloud.

Henry VIII's next step was to abolish the monasteries. The king distributed their lands to his friends and spent their treasuries on wars and luxury. This won the king the support of many powerful English noblemen.

Although Henry VIII established the Church of England as a Protestant church, he would not permit changes to be made to the Catholic doctrine. So he ended up persecuting equally the Catholics who would not go as far as he did, and Protestants who went further. His most famous victim was Sir Thomas More, Renaissance philosopher, author, and the Lord Chancellor of England.

*Above: Catherine of Aragon; below: Anne Boleyn*

As a young man More studied Greek authors and science, absorbing the new spirit of the Renaissance. In 1516, he wrote his famous book *Utopia* – a fictional account of a land inhabited by people whose customs and laws were very different from those of Europe. In *Utopia* More set forth his idea of a perfect society, with just laws and responsible government. The land of Utopia had freedom of religion. No man there was punished for his beliefs. Even atheists were punished only with shaming. In Utopia there were no lawyers because the laws were so simple and clear they needed no interpretation, and because all law-discussing gatherings were open to all. There was no private property in Utopia. Just like in a medieval monastery, where monks owned their property as a commune, all property in Utopia belonged to everyone. Men and women in Utopia were educated alike. Thomas More believed in equality of education. Aware that his wife had not received a good education, he tutored her in music and literature. Later he insisted on giving his daughters the same education as his son. All these ideas were born out of the humanist spirit of the Renaissance, and some were way ahead of their time. Eventually, Thomas More became one of the most prominent English scholars.

However, when it came to the Protestant movement, More took the side of the Catholic Church. He hated Tyndale's translation of the Bible, and believed that some words in that translation were inspired by Protestantism and undermined the authority of the Catholic Church.
For example, the Greek *presbyteros* was translated as 'elder,' rather than 'priest';
the Greek *ekklesia* was translated as 'congregation' rather than 'church';
the Greek *episkopos* was translated as 'overseer,' rather than 'bishop.' Thomas More also rejected the idea of freedom of religion. He started his government career by tracking down and arresting anyone who had Protestant books in their possession. He ordered spying on book publishers and sellers who were suspected of importing Martin Luther's writings in England.

At some point Thomas More became a personal friend of Henry VIII who appointed him Lord Chancellor of England in 1529. As Lord Chancellor, More continued persecuting Protestants and had a few of them burned at the stake as heretics. His agents hunted down William Tyndale and contributed to his capture and death. Henry VIII liked Thomas More's company so much that he kept him at his court and allowed him to go home only once a month. From the palace roof King Henry and Thomas More observed the stars and talked about astronomy. And when More stayed at home, the king would come to dinner uninvited. However, when Thomas More's son-in-law complimented him on the royal friendship, More said, "Trust me, there is no reason to be proud of this. If my head could win the king a castle in France, it would roll."

In *Utopia* Thomas More had given himself a brilliant piece of advice: 'There is no place for philosophy in the councils of kings.' In other words, if you are involved in politics, sooner or later you will have to choose between what is right and what your king wants you to do. Sure enough, soon Thomas More faced that conflict. The king's divorce from Catherine of Aragon had become a huge issue. Sir Thomas believed that the pope was right in refusing to allow it. When it became clear that the king would have his way no matter what, More made his choice. He resigned his office and refused to attend the coronation of Anne Boleyn. Anne was crowned with St Edward's Crown which, until then, had been used only to crown kings. She was the enemy Thomas More could not win against.

Meanwhile the royal couple was not enjoying their marriage. The king spent vast sums of money on Anne Boleyn's bejeweled gowns, ostrich fans, and palace renovations, but Anne was not happy. She was independent and easily annoyed at the rules she had to observe as queen. She had a baby. The king expected a son, an heir to the throne, but the baby was a girl – the future Queen Elizabeth I. It was a huge disappointment. The tournament in honor of the royal birth was canceled. One day Thomas More asked his daughter how things went at the court of Anne Boleyn. "Never better," she responded. "Every day there is dancing and hunting."
"It's painful to think," observed More, "to what a miserable end, poor soul, she will shortly come."

At that point the king's patience with More came to an end. Sir Thomas was accused of taking bribes. His enemies declared that he had received a beautiful golden chalice from a man who won a court case with Thomas More as a judge. More admitted that the man's wife had brought him the golden cup as a New Year's gift. He proved, however, that instead of accepting it, he had filled it with wine, had drunk to the lady's good health, and had given it back. The enemy plot was thwarted.

When the Parliament declared Henry VIII the head of the Church of England, Thomas More's friend, the Duke of Norfolk, tried to convince More to accept King Henry's decision. "It is dangerous to argue with princes," he said. "I wish you inclined somewhat to the king's pleasure."
"Is that all, my Lord?" responded More. "So you think there is no difference between you and me, except that I will die today and you tomorrow?" More refused to take an oath of loyalty to the king as the head of the church, and he also refused to sign the *Oath of Succession* that declared Anne Boleyn's daughter Elizabeth the heir to the English throne. Days later More was imprisoned in the Tower of London. His wife came to see him. She, too, tried to talk him out of arguing with the king. "You've always been a wise man," she said. "But now you act like

a fool, lying here in a filthy prison among mice and rats, instead of being free and comfortable in your own house." "Tell me one thing," said Sir Thomas. "Isn't this prison the same distance to heaven as my own house?" "Tilly-vally, tilly-vally!" responded More's wife. *Tilly-vally* was a 16th-century equivalent of "Bla-bla-bla!"

Sir Thomas More was beheaded in 1535. One of his best known quotes is a joke he made on the scaffold as he kneeled and lay down his head on the execution block. He carefully moved his beard aside to save it from the executioner's axe. "My beard has not offended the king!" he said. Many blamed the death of Thomas More on Anne Boleyn. The following year King Henry's first Queen, Catherine of Aragon, suddenly died. The King and Anne Boleyn celebrated it by wearing yellow – the color of joy – and organizing parties and festivities. Such displays of bad taste made Anne Boleyn even more unpopular. There were rumors that Catherine was poisoned by Anne Boleyn. On top of that, Henry VIII was tired of her.

This time the king didn't bother to ask for divorce. He accused Anne of being unfaithful to him and had her beheaded. As a last gift to Anne, Henry VIII ordered that instead of being beheaded by a common axe, her head should be cut off in a fancy way – by an expert swordsman whom the king invited from France to perform the execution. Anne Boleyn accepted the gift. "I heard the executioner is very good," she said. "And my neck is very slender."

*"The meeting of Sir Thomas More with his daughter after his death sentence" by William Frederick Yeames*

It is believed that a poem that became popular around that time, "O death! rock me asleep..." was written by Anne Boleyn in the Tower:

*O death! rock me asleep,*
*Bring me the quiet rest;*
*Let pass my weary guiltless ghost*
*Out of my care-full breast...*
*Alone in prison strong,*
*I wait my destiny,*
*Woe worth this cruel hap that I*
*Should taste this misery?*

*"First meeting of Henry VIII and Anne Boleyn" by Daniel Maclise*

On the morning of her execution Anne was dressed in a stunning silk dress and a royal mantle of ermine fur. According to witnesses, she looked as happy "as if she was not going to die." She climbed on the execution scaffold and made a speech to the crowd that gathered to see her die. "Good Christian people," she started. "I have come here to die, for according to the law, and by the law I am condemned to die, and therefore I will speak nothing against it." Then she called for God's mercy on those who had sentenced her to death and asked people to pray for the king. Then Anne had a blindfold put over her eyes and was killed with one stroke of the sword while kneeling upright – in the French style of executions.

Ten days later, the king married his third wife, Jane Seymour, who gave birth to his son, the future King Edward VI – and soon died. Next the king thought of proposing to a Protestant German princess Anne of Cleves. The famous court painter, Hans Holbein the Younger, was sent to Germany to paint a portrait of Anne of Cleves for the king. In that portrait she must have looked much better than in real life. When she arrived in London, the king complained to his friends that she looked like a horse. He had their marriage dissolved soon after the wedding. He also executed his new Lord Chancellor, Thomas Cromwell, who had arranged that marriage.

*A portrait of Anne of Cleves, by Hans Holbein the Younger*

On the day of Cromwell's execution the king married Anne Boleyn's cousin Catherine Howard. As a wedding gift Henry gave her the lands of Thomas Cromwell and the jewelry of Anne Boleyn! In no time, however, Catherine Howard was accused of unfaithfulness and beheaded. It became hard to find a new bride for Henry VIII. When the idea of marrying him was suggested to Danish princess Christina, she famously said, "If I had two heads, I would happily contribute one to the King of England." Henry's sixth and last wife, Catherine Parr, outlived him. He died in 1547 at the age of 55.

Thomas More was canonised as a martyr and a saint of the Catholic Church by Pope Pius XI in 1935.

*"Thomas More in prison, visited by his wife and daughter" by Claudius Jacquand; right: Testoon (silver coin) of Henry VIII, 1509*

# NICOLAUS COPERNICUS
## 1473 – 1543

One of the greatest years in the history of science was 1543, when the Polish mathematician and astronomer Nicolaus Copernicus published his book *De revolutionibus orbium coelestium* (Latin for 'On the Revolutions of the Heavenly Spheres'). In his book Copernicus stated that the earth was just a planet revolving around the Sun, not the center of the universe as medieval scholars had believed. Such an idea was considered heretical – contrary to Christian teaching. "If the idea of the earth as the center of the universe were to be given up, then what was man's place in God's creation?" asked church leaders and theologians. They were prepared to defend their medieval beliefs.

Ancient Greek cosmology – the science of the structure and the origin of the universe – suggested that the Earth was a sphere revolving in space – in a *cosmos* – that was also spherical in shape. Pythagoras taught that the Earth revolved around a great central fire. But in the Middle Ages this idea was replaced by the **geocentric** (Earth-centric) theory teaching that the Earth was standing still in space, while the Moon, the Sun, planets, and stars revolved around it. Medieval scholars borrowed this theory from the works of Ptolemy, a 2nd-century astronomer and mathematician who lived in the Roman province of Egypt. His geocentric model of the universe is known as the *Ptolemaic system*. The church identified the Earth as the center of God's creation and rejected as heresy any doubts about its position in the universe.

As a child Copernicus studied Latin and Greek and, along with other Renaissance scientists, rediscovered the scientific knowledge of Ancient Greece. After years of astronomical observations and calculations, it became clear to Copernicus that it was the Earth that revolved around the Sun and not the other way around. So he came up with a *heliocentric* or sun-centered model of the universe (*helios* = Sun in Greek). In *De revolutionibus* he points out that stars seem to move not because they revolve around the Earth, but because the Earth itself moves, revolving around the Sun. Copernicus also calculated that the distance between the Earth and the Sun was much smaller than the distance between the Earth and the stars. Copernicus knew that his ideas would not be accepted by the church, and kept the manuscript of his book to himself, revising and re-revising it year after year until his death. The first copy of his published book is said to have been placed in his hand when he was on his death-bed.

Copernicus' death was the only reason he escaped persecution and trial. Even the new leaders of the Protestant movement who spoke against the dogmas and practices of the Catholic church, believed that the ideas of Copernicus were dangerous. Martin Luther thought Copernicus was a fool to hold such opinions. John Calvin, the founder of the Protestant theology of Calvinism and the leader of the Reformation in Switzerland, wrote: "How could the earth hang suspended in the air if it were not upheld by God's hand? By what means could it stay and not fall down with the heavens above in constant rapid motion, if its Divine Maker had not fixed it in place?"

Some of Copernicus's close friends joined the Protestant movement, but Copernicus remained a devout Catholic. He dedicated his book to Pope Paul III, and in the introduction stated that he had no intention to oppose the teachings of the church. Once his book was published, the ideas of Copernicus were laughed at by the old-school astronomers as the wildest nonsense. But more thoughtful minds carried on his work. And so the scientific Renaissance began.

*"Copernicus, recording the orbits of the stars" by Eduard Ender*

# ST. IGNATIUS OF LOYOLA
## 1491 – 1556

In May 1521, the armies of France and Spain were fighting for the town of Pampeluna. The Spanish garrison inside the city was about to surrender, when a young Spanish knight named Ignatius of Loyola led a successful attack, forcing the French to retreat. A few minutes later, however, a cannonball wounded Ignatius, breaking his right leg. The Spanish fort of Pampeluna fell. But the French noticed and admired the bravery of the young Spanish knight. Following the rules of chivalry, they carried Ignatius to his own home nearby, and the war went on.

Ignatius of Loyola grew up in his father's castle, the youngest of thirteen children. As was the custom in his family, he became a page at the court of Isabella, Queen of Castille. The stories of King Arthur, the knights of Camelot, and of El Cid and his fight against the Muslim invaders, inspired Loyola to seek a military career. He joined the Spanish army at 17. At that time he was far from being a saint. He wasted all his money on fancy clothes and gambling. He danced at parties all night long, and engaged in fights with other knights, occasionally spilling blood. He was rough and arrogant, and there were rumors that he had joined the army to escape being brought to trial for some crime he had committed while drunk during carnival time. Loyola was also an expert swordsman and a good diplomat, but after the Battle of Pampeluna his military career was over.

During the long weeks of his recovery he read the only two books available at his father's castle – *De Vita Christi* – 'About the Life of Christ' by German theologian Ludolph of Saxony, and a biography of saints entitled *Flowers of the Saints*. At first he was bored. But then Loyola noticed that some saints, like St. Francis and St. Dominic, were very much like the knights of the Round Table, except that they fought in a different sort of war, the war against the forces of spiritual darkness. Loyola wondered whether he could endure the hardships and trials experienced by the saints. He began to practice what he afterwards called *spiritual exercises* – a form of Christian meditation. As soon as Loyola could walk again, he headed for a Benedictine monastery in Montserrat. On the way he met a Moor, who was traveling in the same direction. *Moors*, Muslim Arabs of North Africa invaded Spain in the 8th century.

It took Christian Spaniards almost eight centuries to drive the invaders out of Spain. Some Moors, however, stayed and lived peacefully with their Christian neighbors. Loyola and the Moor debated which was the true religion – Christianity or Islam. Loyola was ignorant about theology, so the Moor defeated him easily.

Shaken, Loyola stopped at a local village, bought a piece of prickly worn sackcloth, and made himself a long robe. He also bought a cheap pair of shoes such as those worn by the poorest peasants, obtained a pilgrim's staff, and a gourd to drink from. Arriving at the monastery, Loyola went to confession, and then, like a knight before a battle, he hung his sword before the church altar and kept a vigil, praying until morning. He gave his horse to the monastery, and his fine clothes to a beggar. For a while he lived in a cave, praying seven hours a day, and trying to do what the saints in the books had done – to punish his body for being a source of temptation. He stopped combing his hair and washing his hands. But none of this brought him anywhere closer to God. Then it occurred to Loyola that his body was not his enemy, but his weapon

"Loyola reading" by Albert Chevallier-Tayler in St. Ignatius Church of the Sacred Heart in Wimbledon, England.

in a battle. The best thing he could do with his life was to use it, like a good knight, for the good of others. Loyola was to become neither a hermit, nor a monk, nor a pilgrim, but a teacher of faith.

Ignatius Loyola started his new journey with a pilgrimage. He begged his way to Rome, and then to Venice, and then – by ship – to Jerusalem. He hoped to stay there, but the Franciscan monks who were in charge of Christian services in Jerusalem, discouraged him. They were too poor to add another beggar to their family, and they were also afraid that Loyola would start preaching and anger the Muslim rulers of Jerusalem. So Loyola went to Barcelona and began learning Latin. It was not easy. At 33 he was studying Latin along with school kids . He struggled for two years before he was good enough in Latin to be accepted to the University of Alcala.

While at the university, Loyola tried preaching in public. But one day while he was preaching in the street some women started screaming, rolling on the ground, and behaving as if they were possessed by evil spirits. Loyala was immediately called before the Inquisition. The Inquisition was the judicial tribunal of the Catholic Church, an organization of investigators whose task was to identify heretics and witches. Loyola was locked up in prison, but after a few months they let him go, forbidding him to teach until he spent at least four more years studying theology.

Leaving Alcala, Loyola went to another university, at Salamanca. But the Inquisition was very nervous because of the ideas of Reformation then being spread by Martin Luther, and Loyola's preaching was different from that of other Catholic teachers. So, again, Loyola was imprisoned and chained to a stake on suspicion of heresy. On his release, Loyola went to

*"Loyola begging for alms"*
*by Albert Chevallier-Tayler*

the University of Paris, arriving in France at a moment when the ideas of Protestant Reformation had just started spreading there. One of the strong arguments of Martin Luther against the church of that day was its corruption. No honest person could deny that there was an urgent need for reform. But while Luther chose to leave the Church, Loyola's plan was to reform it from within while defending traditional faith. He dreamed of Catholic renewal, of winning the intellectual battle against both Protestants and Renaissance humanists.

In 1534 a group of seven young men met in the church of Saint Peter, on Montmartre, and under the leadership of Loyola, solemnly vowed to dedicate their lives to

*"Loyola and companions profess their vows" by Albert Chevallier-Tayler*

the ministry he intended to open. Later, they went to Rome where they were ordained into the Catholic priesthood. Loyola organized his group into an order of priests which he named the Society of Jesus – or the *Jesuit* order. The members of the order started traveling with the goal of creating Jesuit schools and seminaries across Europe.

The Latin words *Ite, inflammate omnia* – "Go, set the world on fire" became the motto of these young men. Jesuit colleges started appearing all over. Some attracted more than a thousand students. There were many challenges. Jesuit Peter Canisius described what he found in Vienna: "Not a single priest had been ordained for twenty years; monasteries lay desolate; members of the religious orders were jeered at in the streets; nine-tenths of the inhabitants had abandoned the faith, while the few who still regarded themselves as Catholics had, for the most part, ceased to practice their religion."

In 1540, the society was formally recognized by Pope Paul III. Its rules and methods were set forth in Loyola's book *Spiritual Exercises*. Just like military drills make soldiers, spiritual exercises make saints, taught Loyola. He said that his method of spiritual exercise cures sin like medicine cures a disease. Unlike Protestant thinkers who believed that man has no free will and that salvation is by faith alone, Loyola taught that a person must exercise his free will, and combine faith with good works to achieve salvation. His ideas contributed to a movement of *counter-Reformation* that kept Spain, Italy and France from adopting Protestantism. The Council of Trent that opened in 1545 clarified traditional Catholic doctrine, corrected abuses of power within the church, abolished indulgences, and worked out the strategies of counter-Reformation. By Loyola's death in 1556 the Society of Jesus had grown from seven men to a thousand members in Europe, India, and Brazil.

Loyola's Jesuit brotherhood was unlike any other monastic group. Jesuits did not wear monks' robes. They didn't live in monasteries. They were free to be priests serving parishes, or professors in colleges, or advisors to princes. They were to use all possible means of influence, and practice absolute self-denial and unquestioning obedience to their authorities. "What seems to me white, I will believe black if the hierarchical Church so defines," states Rule XIII from the "Rules for Thinking with the Church" composed by Loyola. Jesuits used the Latin phrase *perinde ac cadaver* – 'like a dead body' – to suggest that the members of their order should be 'dead' to any ideas or ambitions that arise from their own heart or mind. The only acceptable source of philosophy and motivation was the Church.

It is easy to see how such a society looked suspicious to Protestants and Catholics alike. It was a secret society: Nobody knew who belonged to it. Making its way unobserved into politics and education, the Jesuit brotherhood alarmed Europe. The Jesuits were blamed for teaching various evil doctrines, such as the idea that the end justifies the means, or the doctrine of *mental reservation*, which means that you may say one thing aloud, and a very different thing under your breath, and not be blamed for lying.

In 1615 an anonymous author published a book entitled *Monita Secreta* – the 'Secret Instructions' describing methods supposedly used by the members of the Jesuit order. Most historians agree that the document is a fake. However, it caused an uproar when readers found in the book instructions on
- how to undermine the work of other religious orders;
- how to discourage a wealthy widow from another marriage so that she leaves her wealth to the order;
- how to gain the trust of powerful men using information gained from their servants who spy on them;
- how to trap wealthy young men by guilt-tripping, and lure them to join the order...
The Jesuits denied teaching any such things. It is certain that they had no place in the life of Ignatius Loyola. Loyola was canonized by Pope Gregory XV in 1622.

# QUEEN ELIZABETH & MARY, QUEEN OF SCOTS
## 1533 – 1603     1542 – 1587

The reign of Queen Elizabeth I – from 1558 to 1603 – is considered to be the era of the High Renaissance in England. Elizabeth was two years old when her mother Anne Boleyn was sentenced to death and beheaded by her father Henry VIII. When she was 14, Henry VIII died, and Elizabeth's 9-year-old half-brother, Edward VI, became king. Six years later he died too, leaving a will that passed the throne to his 16-year-old cousin Lady Jane Grey. His half-sisters Elizabeth and Mary were excluded from the will. That was the idea of Edward's chief minister, the Duke of Northumberland, who was Lady Jane's father-in-law.

*left: Queen Elizabeth I; below-left: Mary Stuart, Queen of Scots; below-right: 'Bloody Mary' – Mary I, half-sister of Elizabeth*

The Duke of Northumberland tried to keep Edward's death a secret until he could capture and imprison Mary and Elizabeth. But the news reached Mary while she was on her way to visit her sick brother. She took refuge in a castle near the seashore, and sent an order to Parliament to proclaim her queen. The Duke of Northumberland, however, had already offered the crown to Lady Jane Grey.

There was not much cheering at Lady Jane's coronation. Everybody knew that she had no right to the throne, and that Mary was the real queen. But the prospect of Mary's rule was scary. She was poorly-educated, and she was a devout Catholic. The Protestants feared she would restore the Catholic church in England. Elizabeth grew up a Protestant, but she had no chance to become queen while Mary was alive. The Duke of Northumberland had no support and a very small army to uphold Lady Jane Grey. As soon as he had left London with his troops, the Privy Council – the council of royal advisors – persuaded Lady Jane Grey to return home, after a reign of ten days.

Elizabeth's half-sister Mary became queen. She quickly executed the Duke of Northumberland and locked up Elizabeth – first in the Tower and then in a heavily guarded palace. Then she ordered that all the Catholics imprisoned for loyalty to the pope should be set free.

*'Lady Jane Gray is offered the crown' by John Faed*

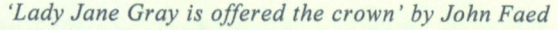

*Prince Philip of Spain*

Mary opened her first Parliament with a public mass. Then she forbade any preaching except by priests loyal to the Catholic Church. Many Protestant reformers were whipped, fined, or imprisoned. Latin masses were again heard in the churches, and many monasteries were given back to the monks.

When Mary married her cousin Prince Philip of Spain, an heir to the Spanish throne, it was a purely political move for both of them. She was 37 and he was 24. Their marriage took place two days after they met. Philip was arrogant, ill-mannered, and treated Queen Mary with contempt. He also pushed her to persecute the reformers. The cruelty of persecutions resulted in a rebellion. The rebels wanted to give the crown back to Lady Jane Grey, but they were defeated. To prevent any more plots, Lady Jane Grey and her husband were sentenced to death. Mary offered to spare her life if she converted to Catholicism, but Lady Jane refused and was beheaded. Three hundred Protestants were burned at the stake as heretics.
Queen Mary was nicknamed Bloody Mary.

Philip soon left Mary and went over to Flanders to wage war. He did not bother to read the long letters she sent him. He needed money for his military campaign, so Mary loaded her people with taxes and sent him all she could. In 1558, when Mary's death was announced in Parliament, members sprang from their seats with shouts of joy, and cries of "God save Queen Elizabeth!" Hearing the news, Elizabeth quoted *Psalm 118* in Latin: *A Domino factum est illud, et est mirabile in oculis notris* – 'It is the Lord's doing, and it is marvelous in our eyes.' Elizabeth was 25 when she became queen. Right away Philip of Spain sent her a proposal of marriage. But Elizabeth was not interested in marrying the nasty husband of her dead half-sister.

One of Elizabeth's first orders was the release of all who were imprisoned for their religion. A group of Protestants came to see the new queen begging her to set free four important prisoners. "What are the names of the captives?" asked Elizabeth. The answer was: "Matthew, Mark, Luke, and John – the four gospel writers. The chain that binds these captives is the Latin language. We want freedom to read the Bible in English."

Elizabeth assembled a council to discuss religious matters, and allowed prayers, hymns, and scriptures in English.

The Church of England, or Anglican Church, was again declared the church of the country, and nine thousand priests were given a choice: Adopt the Anglican services and recognize the queen as the head of the church, or leave the church. Only two hundred left.

Elizabeth was well-educated, generous, and forgiving. But she was also vain, suspicious, and had a violent temper. From time to time there were rumors that the queen was in love with this or that brilliant man at her court. But although Elizabeth loved the admiration and shameless flattery she received, she never accepted any marriage proposals, and was proud of her nickname 'the Virgin Queen.' Some said it was because she didn't want to share power with a husband. Above all Elizabeth loved extravagantly rich dresses and all sorts of luxury. When she died, three thousand spectacular bejeweled gowns and eighty wigs of different colored hair were found hanging in her wardrobes. The queen's manners were coarse. She used a lot of swear words. Despite the floods of praise for her beauty from her court poets, Queen Elizabeth was not a beauty. When she was 29 she had smallpox that left the skin of her face scarred and half of her head bald. Since then she wore wigs and her face was covered in thick layers of makeup. Because she loved candy and was terrified of dentists, she lost many teeth. In one of his reports the French ambassador complained he couldn't understand what the Queen was saying because she was missing so many teeth.

*Queen Elizabeth and her court*

But the common people loved Elizabeth. They would stand for hours waiting to see her leave her palace, and then waved their hats and shouted, 'God save your Majesty!' Elizabeth always stopped and responded: 'God bless you all, my good people.' One day, arriving home, Elizabeth stepped from her coach. Right in front of her was a huge puddle of mud. As she paused, a young man took off his fine cloak, and, bowing low, threw it on the mud before the Queen. Elizabeth invited him to attend her at court. The man was Sir Walter Raleigh, who became a great English explorer, and named one of the first English colonies in America 'Virginia' in honor of the Virgin Queen.

Early in Elizabeth's reign, the pope sent her a message saying that the crown did not really belong to her, because her parents' marriage had not been blessed by the Catholic Church. He ordered her to return to Catholicism. Elizabeth refused. The pope excommunicated her and declared that the English crown belonged to Mary Stuart, the Queen of Scotland and France.

Mary Stuart had become the Queen of Scots when she was only 6 days old. When she was 5 years old, King Henry II of France proposed to unite France and Scotland by marrying the 5-year-old Queen of Scots to his 3-year-old son Francis. The marriage agreement was signed and Mary was sent to France while Scotland was ruled by her mother. At the French court she learned to play the lute, write poetry, and fluently spoke French, Italian, Latin, Spanish, and even Greek, in addition to her native Scots – the Scottish language. In 1559 15-year-old Francis and 16-year-old Mary became king and queen of France. Only a year later Francis died from an ear infection, and Mary returned to Scotland. Scotland was torn between Catholics and Protestants. The teachings of the Reformation had come there from John Calvin, a religious reformer in Geneva, Switzerland. Calvin's student, Scottish Protestant minister John Knox, preached against Mary, who had brought with her to Scotland French tastes, luxury, and a love of dancing. Many Protestants looked upon fashion and dancing as evil.

Queen Elizabeth was jealous of Mary, who was younger and prettier than her. Plus all the Catholics in both kingdoms believed that Mary Stuart should be the Queen of England. So when Mary's life took a tragic turn, Elizabeth had no pity for her. Mary had married her arrogant and nasty cousin Lord Darnley, who was a Catholic. This act offended Scottish Protestant lords. Mary had a son, James, but soon she and her husband broke up. Meanwhile, the Protestant lords formed a plot to get rid of Darnley. They had him murdered. Suspicion fell on Mary and the Earl of Bothwell with whom she was in love. Bothwell shook off accusations, kidnapped Mary and kept her prisoner in his castle until she agreed to marry him.

*"The return of Mary, Queen of Scots, to Edinburgh"* by James Drummond

He had divorced his wife only 12 days before he married Mary in a Protestant wedding ceremony. Scottish Catholics were outraged. Twenty-six Scottish lords turned against Mary and raised their own army. Mary was taken prisoner and locked up in a castle in the middle of the lake Loch Leven. She had to sign a document giving the Scottish crown to her baby son James. Mary made several attempts to escape. Once she bribed a woman who did her laundry to exchange clothes with her, and left the castle in a boat. But she was soon recaptured, betrayed by her own hands that were too white and delicate. Finally she succeeded in escaping, gathered a small army, and marched against her enemies. But her army was defeated, and Mary fled across the border into England, hoping Elizabeth would help her return to the Scottish throne.

Elizabeth, however, viewed Mary as an enemy. She opened a fake investigation into the murder of Lord Darnley, and on the pretext of the investigation Mary was kept prisoner. At first the Queen of Scots received visitors and enjoyed some luxury. But when Elizabeth saw that Mary's beauty, intelligence, and patience won her many friends, she began to grow uneasy. Then a conspiracy was discovered: Catholics were plotting to kill Elizabeth and place Mary on the throne of England. Even though Mary was not found guilty, she was locked up in prison. More conspiracies followed – Catholics kept trying to set Mary free.

Finally, in 1587, after she had been imprisoned for 19 years, Mary was tried for plotting against Elizabeth, and sentenced to death as a traitor. On the day of her execution Mary Stuart was wearing her best royal dress. In one hand she carried a Bible, in the other a crucifix. Her hair was gray. Executioners knelt before her asking for her pardon, and she forgave them. The next day Elizabeth wore black and fired one of her advisors. She claimed she had recalled the death warrant, but her advisors had gone ahead and executed Mary anyway.

*Right: Official portrait of Queen Elizabeth I; below: "Robert Devereux, 2nd Earl of Essex, arrives uninvited to see Queen Elizabeth and finds her with no wig or makeup" by David Wilkie Wynfield*

Mary's son James, who was now the King of Scotland, hated Elizabeth, but he had neither the money nor the soldiers to fight against England, so he did nothing. Elizabeth hoped that finally the troubles from the Catholics were over. She was wrong! Mary had left a will in which she said she was passing the throne of England to Philip of Spain! By that time he had become the King of Spain. In the harbor of Cadiz Philip gathered a huge fleet that came to be known as the Great Armada. The fleet was to sail to England and overthrow Elizabeth. Elizabeth started preparing for war. Along their South Coast the English built a system of beacons to quickly deliver the news of an invasion to London. Elizabeth's greatest helper at this time was one of her bravest seamen, Sir Francis Drake. He had made voyages to America, had captured several gold-laden Spanish galleons, and was the first Englishman to see the Pacific and sail around the globe. With thirty small ships, Francis Drake sailed into the Spanish harbor of Cadiz, and destroyed the ships and supplies King Philip was preparing for the invasion of England. The sailing of the Armada was delayed until the following year.

Finally, the 130-ship Spanish Armada sailed northward. It was spotted near Cornwall by a Scottish pirate. Signal fires were soon lit on hilltops all along the coast. The English allowed the Armada to pass by, but then followed it up the English Channel. As the English ships approached, the Armada took a crescent-shaped defensive formation. The Spanish galleons were heavy and slow. They were crowded with soldiers and relied on using grappling hooks to trap enemy ships, board them, and set them on fire. The English ships were light and fast, and manned by more skilful seamen and better gunners. They stayed out of grappling range and bombarded the Spanish Armada with cannon fire. Seeing their ships catch fire one by one, the Spanish fled North, hoping to return to Spain by sailing around the British Isles. However, a severe tempest wrecked most of the Armada ships along the Irish coast. Only fifty-three vessels made it back to Spain. The defeat of the Armada freed the English from their fear of Spain. It inspired national pride, and the foundations were soon laid for a great colonial empire based on naval power that made England "the mistress of the seas."

*The burning of the Spanish Armada*

The flourishing of arts during the reign of Elizabeth I is often called the *Elizabethan Age*. Great poets and playwrights such as William Shakespeare, Christopher Marlowe, and Edmund Spenser, brought the spirit of the Renaissance into English literature and theater.

For centuries the Elizabethan era would be considered the golden age of English history both by scholars and the anonymous authors of street ballads like *The Golden Days of Good Queen Bess*:

*Then our streets were unpaved, our houses were thatched, sir,*
*Our windows were latticed, our doors only latched, sir,*
*Yet so few were the rogues that would plunder or rob, sir,*
*That the hangman was starved for want of a job, sir.*
*Oh, the golden days of good Queen Bess!*

Shortly before her death Elizabeth was asked to appoint an heir to the English throne. She said, "I will have no rascal's son in my seat, but one worthy to be a king." And she gave the English crown to Mary Stuart's son James. James had been raised a Protestant.

*Mid-16th-century hand gun*

*"Queen Elizabeth offers the crown of England to Mary Stuart's son James" by Paul Delaroche; right: King James I of England*

# WILLIAM SHAKESPEARE
## 1564 – 1616

Among all the writers of the Elizabethan era, William Shakespeare stands first. He was born into a poor family in Stratford on the river Avon, in 1564. He received a grammar school education, got married at 18, and went to London, where he became an actor and writer of plays. He is considered to be the greatest playwright and poet of modern times. His 154 sonnets, 34 plays and two epic poems have been translated into all major languages. Because of the enormous influence of Shakespeare on English literature and language, there are dozens of everyday sayings that come from Shakespeare's plays. For example:

- *have/has seen better days* = in bad condition, worn out (from *As You Like It*, Act 2 Scene 7)
- *too much of a good thing* = you stop to appreciate or enjoy things you do too often (from *As You Like It*, Act 4 Scene 1)
- *neither rhyme nor reason* = makes no sense (from *The Comedy of Errors*, Act 2 Scene 2)
- *in my heart of hearts* = about deep, true feelings (from *Hamlet*, Act 3 Scene 2)
- *the be-all and the end-all* = the definitive and final example (from *Macbeth*, Act 1 Scene 7)
- *what's done is done* = you cannot change the past (from *Macbeth*, Act 3 Scene 2)
- *a foregone conclusion* = the inevitable result (from *Othello*, Act 3 Scene 3)
- *all that glitters isn't gold* = sometimes things are not as good as they appear to be (from *The Merchant of Venice*, Act 2 Scene 7)
- *the world is my oyster* = I can achieve whatever I want to in life (from *The Merry Wives of Windsor*, Act 2)
- *wild-goose chase* = a hopeless search (from *Romeo and Juliet*, Act 2 Scene 4)
- *to break the ice* = to start a conversation, to make people feel at ease (from the *Taming of the Shrew*, Act 1 Scene 2)
- *brave new world* = a new, better situation (from *The Tempest*, Act 5 Scene 1)
- *to melt into thin air* = to disappear without a trace (from *The Tempest*, Act 4 Scene 1)

*Miniature portrait, England, 1588*

Shakespeare's plays were performed by a London theater company owned by a group of actors, including Shakespeare. It was so successful that it became the leading theater in London, known as 'The King's Men.' In 1599 the company built their own theater named the Globe.

How could a poor kid with only a grammar school education have such perfect command of sophisticated literary language and such a deep knowledge of Renaissance high culture, including European history, Greek and Roman mythology and literature? There was no library in Stratford-on-Avon that could have had all the books that young Shakespeare needed to read to achieve that level of education. Also, Shakespeare's plays and poems reveal that the author was familiar with astronomy, medicine, with the manners and customs of royal courts, with military life, with travel around Europe, and with aristocratic sports like archery, hunting, falconry, and tennis. But Shakespeare, supposedly, was a poor actor who never left England. Legal documents signed by Sheakespeare's daughters seem to have primitive marks instead of real signatures. How could his daughters be illiterate, if the female characters of Shakespeare's plays write letters, poetry, and display a high level of education? Shakespeare's own signatures on legal documents look like scribblings of a barely literate man.

In Shakespeare's will he mentions his second-best bed (!), but there is no mention of books he may have owned, or even of his own manuscripts, including the 18 plays that were still unpublished at the time of his death. And more: The epitaph carved on Shakespeare's gravestone is a junky poem that could be written by a 3rd-grader. Could this have been composed by one of the greatest poets of all times?

*Good friend, for Jesus' sake, forebear*
*To dig the dust enclosed here.*
*Blessed be the man who spares these stones,*
*and cursed be he, who moves my bones.*

In light of all this, many scholars question the authorship of Shakespeare. They claim that the works attributed to him were actually written by someone else. The real author of those poems and plays must have had a spectacular Renaissance humanist education. Could it be a poet from aristocratic circles who used the name of one of the actors to hide his identity? Being a playwright was not considered appropriate for an educated person. Scholars have named many candidates for 'the real Shakespeare.' Here are some of them.

*Above: William Stanley, Edward de Vere;*
*below: Christopher Marlowe*

## 1. Edward de Vere, 17th Earl of Oxford

Edward de Vere was a classically-educated courtier, poet, and one of the favorites of Queen Elizabeth. He was also a patron of theater, and wrote plays, although he never signed them with his own name. Edward de Vere traveled extensively in Italy and France – locations often described in Shakespeare's plays, where Shakespeare himself never traveled. In the Bible that belonged to de Vere many passages are underlined. These passages are quoted in Shakespeare's plays! His coat of arms features a lion holding – or 'shaking' – a spear! Characters in Shakespeare's play *Hamlet* resemble some members of De Vere's family. And it was De Vere's family that funded the publication of the first volume of Shakespeare's works in 1623. Shakespeare's plays hint at many events – political and cultural – that happened during his lifetime, but there are no mentions of events that happened after the death of Edward de Vere! Two of Shakespeare's plays have quotations from the first page of a Latin grammar textbook which every boy of Shakespeare's time knew by heart. As an example of proper nouns, that page offers the following sentence: *Edwardus is my proper name*. Was that a hint at Edward de Vere's authorship?

*Left: De Vere's signature; right: Shakespeare's signature; below: Will Derby's signature*

## 2. Poet and playwright Christopher Marlow

Marlowe was from a simple family, just like Shakespeare, but he was educated at Cambridge University, and was famous for his plays, especially *Doctor Faustus*. Marlowe was one of the first English poets to use *blank verse* – poetry where lines don't rhyme – which became a signature style of Shakespeare's plays. Computer analysis shows an extreme similarity between the writing styles of Marlowe and Shakespeare. Either Shakespeare was inspired by Marlowe's poetry, or maybe Marlow didn't die in a tavern fight at the age of 29... Some scholars believe Christopher Marlowe faked his own death to avoid being charged, condemned, and executed as an atheist. Shakespeare's first published work came out two weeks after Marlowe's death!

## 3. William Stanley, 6th Earl of Derby

William Stanley was a patron of theater companies. A Jesuit spy who kept an eye on him wrote in his report in 1599 that Stanley was "busy penning comedies for common players." Shakespeare referred to himself in his sonnets as *Will*. William Stanley went by 'Will Derby.' Also, notice, his initials were *W.S.* – the same as William Shakespeare's! William Stanley traveled a lot in continental Europe, including Navarre, where Shakespeare's play *Love's Labour's Lost* is set.

# King Henry IV of France
## 1553 – 1610

The last decades of the Renaissance in France were the reign of King Henry IV. Henry IV – or Henry of Navarre – was born in the south of France, in Navarre. His mother, Jeanne, the Queen of Navarre, had him brought up together with peasant children, to teach him how to handle hardships and be independent. For a cradle he had a large turtle shell. Growing up, he ran wild with the kids from the nearby village and ate peasant food – black bread and beef with garlic. Henry's mother was a Protestant. She made Protestantism the religion of Navarre. French protestants who followed the teaching of Swiss reformer John Calvin called themselves the *Huguenots*.

When Henry was 15 his mother brought him to the camp of the Huguenot army fighting against French Catholics. Standing before the troops he announced, "Your cause is mine, your interests are mine; I swear on my soul, honour and life, to be wholly yours." He became the commander of the Huguenots, and at 19 the King of Navarre. Henry's mother had arranged a marriage for him: Henry was to marry Margaret of Valois, daughter of King Henry II

*"Jeanne of Navarre buys poisoned gloves from Catherine de' Medici's perfume supplier"* by Pierre-Charles Comte

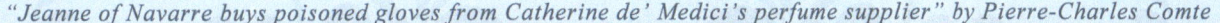

was long dead and Catherine de' Medici ruled France on behalf of her son, King Charles IX, who spent his days hunting and had no idea what was going on in his kingdom. Catherine decided to bring Navarre under her influence, and Henry's mother Queen Jeanne agreed to the marriage on the condition that Henry could remain a Huguenot. However, she died two months before Henry's wedding. Her courtiers suspected she had been poisoned by Catherine de' Medici, using a pair of perfumed gloves soaked in poison.

In 1572 Henry went to Paris for his wedding. Thousands of Huguenots were invited to Paris to celebrate his marriage. Meanwhile Catherine de' Medici, who hated Protestants, convinced her son, King Charles, that the Huguenots were about to rebel. The day after the wedding was August 24 – the Feast of St. Bartholomew. Between one and two in the morning a bell rang out in the stillness of the summer night. It was the signal for Catholics to attack the Huguenots in Paris. The moment the single bell sounded, every bell in Paris echoed it. Armed men with torches and white crosses on their sleeves flooded the city and put to death every Huguenot they could find – men, women, and children. That night thousands of Huguenots in Paris and throughout France were killed. In Rome, a thanksgiving service was held because so many heretics had been destroyed. All Europe was shaken at the terrible massacre of St. Bartholomew's Day, and no king, except King Philip II of Spain, praised that horrible act. Henry of Navarre narrowly escaped death. He was forced to promise that he would convert to Catholicism and was kept at the royal court as a prisoner. After that day Charles IX had no peace of mind. To escape the feeling of guilt, he spent twelve or fourteen hours every day hunting.

*"Catherine de' Medici on the morning after the St. Bartholomew massacre" by Edouard Debat-Ponsan*

In 1574, after two unhappy years, Charles fell ill and died. Henry III, brother of Charles IX, became king. Meanwhile Henry of Navarre escaped from Paris. He went hunting, but instead of returning to the palace, he rode away. His marriage didn't last – he and his wife Margaret had separated soon after the wedding. Now, again, he was the commander of the Huguenots. In 1576, scared of the Huguenots' growing military power, Catherine de' Medici advised the king to make a treaty with them. That angered French Catholics. Led by the Duke of Guise, they formed an army called the Holy League and rebelled against the king. A civil war broke out – the 'War of the Three Henries ' – King Henry III, Henry, King of Navarre, and Henry, Duke of Guise.

Unable to defeat the Holy League, Henry III asked Henry of Navarre for help. Together they lay siege to Paris, which was held by the League. Catholics were outraged that the King of France had made friends with a Huguenot to save his crown. Priests in Paris called for Henry III to be assassinated. One young monk left the city, came to Henry III's camp and asked to talk to the king, saying he had a secret message for him. He was admitted to the king's presence, and when he came close, he drew a dagger from his sleeve and stabbed the king. Henry III died the next morning, leaving the throne to Henry of Navarre – now Henry IV. In Paris there was great joy when it became known that the king was dead. Bells rang, bonfires blazed. But Henry of Navarre did not have enough support to take the city and claim the crown. The League was stronger than ever. Some Catholics agreed to fight for him. "You are not the king of Catholics or Huguenots. You are the king of the brave," they said. But most Catholics refused to accept him as king. "Better die than endure a heretic king, " they murmured.
In his own words Henry IV was now "a king without a kingdom, a husband without a wife, and a warrior without money."

Despite many setbacks, in 1590 Henry won an important battle against the Holy League – the Battle of Ivry, which became the turning point in his life. Before the battle they brought to Henry a prisoner, a captured Holy League Catholic. Henry happened to know him, and embraced him like a friend. Looking at Henry's army the prisoner thought it seemed much smaller than the army of the Holy League. "Where are your forces?" he asked Henry. "You don't see all our forces," Henry replied. "You haven't counted God and the rightfulness of my cause, but they are always with me."

Henry also had the help of German protestants. On the eve of the Battle of Ivry, the Baron of Schomberg, leader of a band of German troops, came to Henry IV asking for money for his men. Irritated, Henry answered: "Men of honor do not ask for money on the eve of battle!" But the next morning, realizing how unjust he had been, he walked up to the baron in front of

*"Henry IV enters Paris"* by Francois Gerard

his whole army, and apologized, saying: "Baron, I insulted you yesterday. This may be the last day of my life, and I would not willingly take away with me the honor of a gentleman. Pardon me, and embrace me." "It's true," responded the baron, "yesterday Your Majesty wounded me with your words but to-day I will lay down my life in your service!" Addressing his soldiers, Henry said: "My friends, keep your ranks in good order, and follow the white plume on my helmet that will lead you to honor and glory!" At some point on the battlefield Henry's men started to retreat, but Henry saved the day by yelling at them, "Turn around, you cowards, and if you won't fight, at least see me die!"

Henry's army grew. Queen Elizabeth of England sent him money to pay his soldiers. Encouraged with the victory at Ivry, Henry besieged Paris and held it for four months under strict blockade. During the last two months many people in the city died of hunger. Henry felt bad for the people trapped in Paris. He allowed some food to be sent to them, and let six thousand old men, women and children leave the city. "Paris must not become a cemetery," he told his generals. "I do not wish to reign over the dead." The suburbs were soon in Henry's hands, but just as Paris was about to surrender, the Spanish King Philip II decided it was time to interfere. He sent an army of mercenaries to defend the city. When it became clear that victory over the Spanish would cost a great loss of life and destruction, Henry quietly withdrew. "I would rather not have Paris at all," he said, "than to see it all torn to pieces and dead."

Now Henry IV realized that without Catholic support he could not win the crown of France.

Could it be time to become a Catholic? Henry asked a Protestant minister: "Do you believe a man can be saved by the Catholic religion?" The minister responded: "Undoubtedly, if his life and heart be holy." "Then," said the king, "I should embrace the Catholic religion, and not yours. If I am Catholic, then, according to both Catholics and Protestants, I may be saved, but if I am a Protestant, I shall not be saved according to the Catholics."

His famous words "Paris is well worth a mass!" summed up his decision. He went to the Abbey of St. Denis and knocked on the door. The bishop of the abbey opened, asking, "Who are you?"
"The king," answered Henry.
"What do you seek?"
"To be received into the fold of the Catholic,

*A portrait of Marie de' Medici by Frans Pourbus and a French Renaissance gold and enamel pendant*

Apostolic, Roman Church." Then, kneeling, Henry declared: "I swear, in the presence of God Almighty, to live and die in the Catholic faith, and to protect and defend it against all, at the peril of my life and blood!" The bishop granted him absolution of sins, and led him into the church, where mass was celebrated. Henry's next move was to be solemnly crowned in the cathedral at Chartres. Most of the Catholics were now willing to obey him, and a few months later the gates of Paris opened to him, and he entered his capital without striking a blow. Parisians were so happy that they crowded around him, shouting and congratulating him. Within the next two years, Henry became the master of all France. The towns he did not conquer, he bought with bribes. In 1598 he signed the Edict of Nantes, which gave Protestants the right to practice their religion, and gave them the same rights as the Catholics.

Henry had his first marriage annulled, and married Marie de' Medici, a niece of Catherine de' Medici. The Medici helped Henry finance his military campaigns and for eight years put pressure on him to marry Marie. Marie looked charming in a portrait the Medici had sent to the king, so he married her *by proxy*. A marriage *by proxy* is a wedding where either bride groom, or both, are absent, and are represented by a friend or family member. In Henry IV and Marie de' Medici's wedding Henry was represented by the bride's uncle, the Grand Duke Ferdinand of Tuscany. Ferdinand put the wedding ring on Marie's finger and she was pronounced the wife of the French King. When Henry finally met Marie he was disappointed. She looked completely different from her portrait and had a violent temper, easily getting worked up over nothing. Henry's friends hated her and called her "the fat bankeress of Florence." But there was no going back. The royal couple managed to save their relationship and had six children.

*"King Henry IV and Marie de' Medici" by Wladyslaw Bakalowicz; below: "Assassination of Henry IV" by Charles-Gustave Housez*

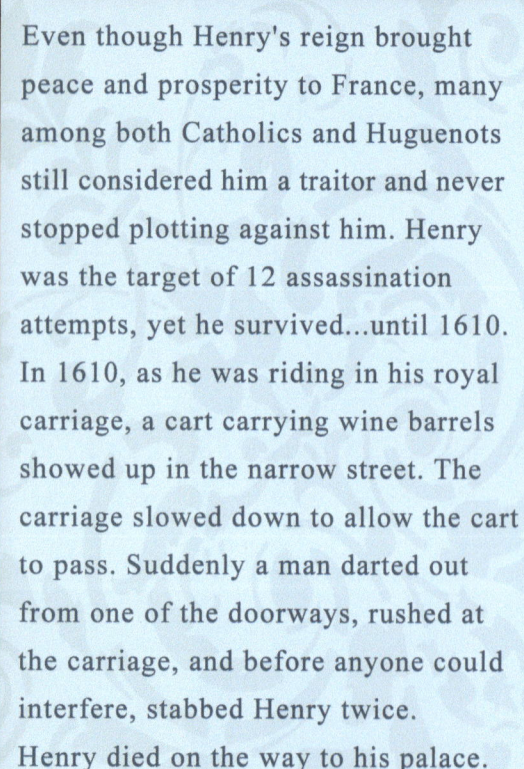

Even though Henry's reign brought peace and prosperity to France, many among both Catholics and Huguenots still considered him a traitor and never stopped plotting against him. Henry was the target of 12 assassination attempts, yet he survived...until 1610. In 1610, as he was riding in his royal carriage, a cart carrying wine barrels showed up in the narrow street. The carriage slowed down to allow the cart to pass. Suddenly a man darted out from one of the doorways, rushed at the carriage, and before anyone could interfere, stabbed Henry twice. Henry died on the way to his palace.

# NOSTRADAMUS
## 1503 – 1566

Nostradamus was a French Renaissance astrologer and doctor who became famous for his prophecies about the future. Nostradamus is the Latin name of Michel de Nostredame. He started his career as a pharmacist and doctor. His wife and two children died of plague, and Nostradamus fought against all odds to save others from the deadly disease. Along the way Nostradamus started working as an astrologer for wealthy patrons. His most prominent admirer was Catherine de' Medici. In 1555 he published his book *Les Propheties* ('The Prophecies'), a collection of short poems predicting various future events.

The book was such a hit it has never been out of print since its publication. Renaissance history is full of horrific events – plagues, invasions, civil wars, floods, droughts, massacres, assassinations, mass executions, and so on. It is not surprising that the people of the Renaissance era always expected that there were more disasters to come. Collections of end-of-the-world prophecies were a popular genre of literature. The fans of Nostradamus claim he had supernatural abilities and credit him with predicting major historical events of the distant future – such as the rise of Hitler, the invention of the atomic bomb, and the 9/11 Muslim terrorist attack on the World Trade Center in New York City.

Sceptics say Nostradamus was no better than any fortune-teller, that his predictions are vague, and could easily be applied to any event. He gave no specific dates. His opponents say his fame as a 'seer' of the future is merely due to misinterpretations and mistranslations of his book. A lot of the material in *Les Propheties* is borrowed from other medieval and Renaissance books of prophecies, such as *Mirabilis liber* ('Miraculous book') published in 1522 – a collection of prophecies by Christian saints. Nostradamus translated them from Latin and retold them in French. He also clearly believed that history repeated itself, and 'predicted' events described by Classical Greek and Roman authors. Nostradamus himself denied having any gift of prophecy. In the introduction to his book and also in his personal letters he states "I am not foolish enough to claim to be a prophet." Still, the mystery of Nostradamus has fascinated the world ever since *Les Propheties*. Here are some passages from his book that have made people from the 16th century to this day believe Nostradamus.

*The young lion will overcome the older one on the field of combat in a single battle;*
*He will pierce his eyes through a golden cage. Two wounds made one, then he dies a cruel death.*
Nostradamus believers claim that in this poetic stanza Nostradamus was predicting the death of King Henry II of France. King Henry died from a wound caused by a fragment of lance that pierced his eye through his helmet.

Fans of Nostradamus say the following poem from Les Propheties predicted the great fire of London that destroyed most of the medieval city in 1666.
*The blood of the just will be demanded of London burnt by fire in the year '66*
*The ancient Lady will fall from her high place, and many of the same sect will be killed.*

Did Nostradamus predict the French Revolution of 1789 in the following lines?
*From the enslaved populace, songs, chants and demands*
*While princes and lords are held captive in prisons.*
*These will, in the future, by headless idiots, be received as divine prayers.*

They say that the following poem by Nostradamus predicted the rise of Hitler:
*From the depths of the West of Europe a young child will be born of poor people.*
*He who by his tongue will seduce a great troop.*
*His fame will increase towards the realm of the East.*

The following poem is said to have predicted the USA dropping atomic bombs on Hiroshima and Nagasaki in 1945.
*Near the gates and within two cities*
*There will be scourges the like of which was never seen,*
*Famine within plague, people put out by steel*
*crying to the great immortal God for relief.*

*Gilded silver chalice, France, 1532*

Some people believe this poem predicted Neil Armstrong's landing on the moon in 1969:
*He will come to travel to the corner of Luna where he will be captured and put in a strange land,*
*The unripe fruits to be subject of great scandal, great blame – to one, great praise.*

Was the following poem a prediction of the Muslim tererorist attack on New York City on 9/11?
*Earthshaking fire from the center of the Earth will cause tremors around the New City.*
*Two great rocks will war for a long time. Then Arethusa will redden a new river.*

# Galileo Galilei & Giordano Bruno
## 1563 – 1642　　　　　　　　　1548 – 1600

The stars of the Scientific Renaissance are often called the 'heroes of thought.' They fought an unequal battle with fanatical defenders of the old medieval worldview. When astronomers – such as Copernicus – started questioning the geocentric model of the universe, ignorant theologians of the day felt they were attacking the very foundations of religion. The Inquisition – the heretic-hunters of the Catholic Church – targeted scientists whose ideas seemed to them contrary to Scripture. Quite a few brave men of science lost their lives burned at the stake as heretics on the squares of Europe. One of them was Giordano Bruno, a Neapolitan monk and an astronomer. Persecuted and hunted from place to place, he was at last seized by the Inquisition, and after eight years of imprisonment was burned as a heretic.

*Galileo Galilei*

*Giordano Bruno*

"There is no reason," he said, "that the Earth holds a high rank among the stars. It is time to dethrone it! Let this not discourage man, let him not think he is forsaken by God. For if God is everywhere, if there is, in truth, an unnumbered host of stars and suns, why would the difference between the Earth and the Heavens matter at all? Inhabitants of a world around a star, are we not included in the celestial realm set at the very gates of Heaven?"
Sayings such as these cost Bruno his life. He dared to break the bonds of "authority," to think for himself, and to follow truth – even to death.

The new day dawned on Europe slowly and stormily. But in spite of the heavy hand of superstition, in spite of dark prisons, torture, and public executions, the movement of the Scientific Renaissance grew until the old order vanished, and a new order took its place all over Western Europe. In every country, on all subjects, men fought for and won the right of private judgment, the right of individual freedom.

Probably the most famous Renaissance hero of science is Galileo Galilei. His family was from Florence, but they lived in Pisa, the town famous for its great leaning tower. Galileo's father, a wool merchant, was highly-educated. He wrote books as a hobby. After elementary school Galileo was sent to a monastery to study literature and arts. In Medieval Europe monasteries were the centers of education, and after the capture of Constantinople by the Turks in 1453, many Greek scholars from Byzantium found refuge in European monasteries, bringing with them their libraries and the tradition of studying classical Greek and Roman sources.
Next Galileo went to the University to study medicine. By the time he was 20, Galileo was an excellent Latin and Greek scholar, as well as an accomplished artist and musician. However his teachers disliked his questioning spirit – a warning of what lay ahead for Galileo.

While still a university student, Galileo made a discovery when sitting in the Pisa Cathedral. He noticed that a large hanging lamp was set in motion when it was lit, and kept swinging like a pendulum. Over time its swings were becoming shorter and shorter. Galileo noticed that the chandelier took almost the same time for each swing, no matter how far it was swinging. Based on that observation Galileo invented a device a doctor could use to measure a patient's pulse.

While studying medicine Galileo became interested in mathematics. But doctors were paid higher salaries than mathematicians, so Galileo's father prohibited him from taking classes in math. One day, visiting a friend of the family who tutored children at the Court of Tuscany, Galileo overheard him conduct a class in geometry. Galileo stood hiding by the half-opened door to the end of the class. For days he kept returning and hiding there, until he had heard the entire course. After that experience, there was no turning back. Galileo persisted in his studies. At 25 he was appointed to the chair of mathematics at the University of Pisa.

Soon the scholars of Pisa were shocked, as Galileo questioned some of the theories of Aristotle. Aristotle, one of the greatest ancient Greek philosophers, was an absolute authority to the scholars of the Middle Ages. If a scholar referred to Aristotle to support his opinion, he automatically won a debate. Quotes of Aristotle were accompanied by the Latin phrase *magister dixit* –

*The Leaning Tower of Pisa*

'the teacher has spoken' – that signalled an end to any further discussion. But Aristotle's writings contain a lot of statements that are, by modern standards, unscientific, or plain wrong. In one of his works, it is said that the heavier an object is, the faster it falls down. This was wrong, declared Galileo, and offered to disprove Aristotle's statement by an experiment. University professors and students alike laughed at Galileo. But he invited them to the leaning tower of Pisa and dropped two weights – a ten-pound weight and a one-pound weight – from the top floor of the tower. The weights would hit the ground together, predicted Galileo. University professors were nearly bursting from laughter: They knew that, according to Aristotle, the heavier weight would reach the ground first! Picture them in total disbelief when they heard a loud thud and saw the two weights land on the ground simultaneously!

Some years later Galileo moved to the University of Padua. His fame as a mathematician spread, and many foreign scholars and princes came to Padua to be present at his lectures. Meanwhile, in 1604, the scientific world was marveling at the sudden appearance of a new star. Night after night its brilliant light, changing from orange to yellow, purple, red, and white illumined the sky. Galileo studied it, and his lecture rooms were crowded when it was announced that he would give a public explanation of that wonder. The followers of Aristotle believed that the new star was a meteor, that it was nearer the earth than the moon. It couldn't be a star, they argued, because one of the axioms of Aristotle was the "incorruptibility of the heavens." The universe was unchangeable and perfect, taught Aristotle. Nothing could be added to it or taken away from it. The stars were carried in hollow crystalline spheres around the Earth. They couldn't just appear or disappear. But Galileo proved by exact calculations that the new star was much farther from the Earth than the Sun and it couldn't be a meteor. Today we know that the star of 1604 was a supernova explosion 20,000 light years from the Earth.

In June, 1609, a rumor reached Galileo that a Dutch optician in Middleburg invented "an instrument for increasing the apparent size of remote objects." It was a funny optical toy – two lenses mounted on a stand. When you looked through them, you could see the weather-vane on a distant church much nearer – though upside down. The optical toy set Galileo thinking. A similar device could help him study stars and planets. Inspired, he constructed the first real telescope. It offered only x3 magnification, but Galileo kept improving his invention and eventually reached x30 magnification. Using his telescope he discovered Jupiter's moons, and learned that the Milky Way consisted of stars – not of clouds as was previously believed. He also observed the phases of Venus and realized that it was possible to see them only if Venus revolved around the Sun! He concluded that Copernicus was right: The Earth was not the center of the Universe.

That idea was considered heresy by the church. So in his lectures Galileo still taught that the Sun and planets revolved around the Earth. However, in a letter to Kepler, another great mathematician of that era, he wrote: "Many years ago I became a convert to the opinions of Copernicus, and by that theory have succeeded in fully explaining many phenomena which on the contrary hypothesis are altogether inexplicable. I have come up with many arguments which, however, I have not so far dared to publish, for fear of sharing the fate of our teacher, Copernicus, who, although he has earned immortal fame with some, yet with very many (so great is the number of fools) has become an object of ridicule and scorn."

Galileo's telescopes became a sensation. His house was crowded with visitors eager to see "Galileo's tube." Astronomical observatories were besieged with people who demanded to look at the sky through a telescope. One was sent to Paris, to Marie de' Medici, King Henry IV's wife. When the telescope was brought to the Louvre, Marie was so eager to use it that she did not wait for the instrument to be lifted onto a window sill, but went down on her knees before the window, which greatly astonished the Italians who had brought her the telescope.

What did the professors of the old geocentric school have to say about Galileo's discoveries? Jupiter's satellites don't exist, they claimed. There are only seven openings in the head – two eyes, two ears, two nostrils, and one mouth. There are only seven metals, and only seven days in the week, therefore there can be only seven planets: Two 'favorable' – Venus and Jupiter; two 'unfavorable' – Mars and Saturn; two luminaries – the Sun and the Moon; and Mercury that was 'undecided.' They also argued that the new planets could not exist because Aristotle had made no mention of them.

One of Galileo's students, Benedetto Castelli was a professor of mathematics at the University of Pisa. Castelli was forbidden to teach the heliocentric system, but one day he went to a dinner party hosted by Grand Duchess Christina of Florence, and at the party he was dragged into a discussion about the two models of the universe – geocentric and heliocentric.

The Duchess claimed that Copernicus' theory contradicts the Bible. Castelli defended it and his arguments were so convincing that all the guests agreed with him, not with the Duchess. Castelli described this incident in a letter to Galileo, and Galileo responded with a letter that got him into trouble with the church. Galileo's main point was that "the Bible was intended to teach us not how the heavens go, but how to go to heaven."

In 1615, Galileo's letter to Castellini and other writings defending Copernicus' theory were submitted to the Roman Inquisition. The Inquisition officially declared the heliocentric model of the universe 'heretical,' 'foolish,' 'absurd,' and contrary to the teaching of the Bible. Galileo went to Rome to confront theologians about his discoveries. However, Pope Paul V, who was a supporter of Galileo, ordered him to abandon heliocentric theory and never teach it again in any form. Copernicus's *De Revolutionibus* and other heliocentric works were banned. For about 10 years Galileo stayed away from arguments about the structure of the universe.

Pope Paul V died in 1623 and a new Pope, Urban VIII, was elected. A friend and a fan of Galileo, Urban VIII wrote about the heliocentric system: "The Church has not condemned this system; and it should not be condemned as heretical, but only as not well-researched." With the blessing of the pope Galileo started writing a book about the two systems – heliocentric and geocentric – *Dialogue Concerning the Two Chief World Systems*. Urban VIII suggested that Galileo should describe both systems but not take the side of Copernicus. However, the arguments in favor of the heliocentric system in Galileo's book were too convincing.

Some members of the Jesuit order, long-time enemies of Galileo, put pressure on the Pope's office to stop the publication of his book. Galileo's publisher was ordered to cease printing the book and to send to Rome all copies he had in his possession. But by that time there was not a single copy left – they had all been sold!

*'Galileo faces inquisition'* – painting by Cristiano Banti

*"Galileo before the Holy Office"* by Joseph-Nicolas Robert-Fleury

Three weeks later Galileo arrived in Rome and was brought before the dreaded Inquisition. It is to the Pope's credit that during the trial he did not allow Galileo to be treated as an ordinary prisoner. He was never placed in a prison cell, but stayed at the Embassy of Florence or in the building of the Holy Office. His doors were not even required to be locked. Galileo's friend the Ambassador of Florence advised him not to defend himself, but to admit his 'guilt.' Galileo was commanded to deny the heliocentric theory. So, standing on his knees, with the hand on the Bible, he declared: "I do not hold, and have not held, this opinion of Copernicus since I was ordered to abandon it. For the rest I am here in your hands; do with me as you please." The popular story is that having admitted that the Earth stands still in the middle of the universe, Galileo rose from his knees and muttered, "And yet it moves."

The Inquisition felt that it was necessary to pronounce the sentence of perpetual imprisonment. However, Galileo was allowed to live in his own villa and receive visitors until his death in 1642. Although copies of Galileo's statement rejecting the heliocentric system were immediately circulated throughout Italy, and were ordered to be read in the universities, the Copernican system still kept its hold upon the minds of all advanced thinkers, and Galileo was still regarded as its most powerful advocate. He was not tortured and sentenced to death like Jordano Bruno, but the ban on his publishing and science work made him bitter. In one of Galileo's letters he admitted he was tempted to burn his research papers: "I feel even the desire to destroy forever, to commit to the flames, whatever of my work remains in my hands – to satisfy the burning hate of my enemies. These thoughts cause me physical suffering, and never-ending insomnia."

The malice of Galileo's enemies followed him to the end, and he was denied the right of making a will, and of burial in consecrated ground.

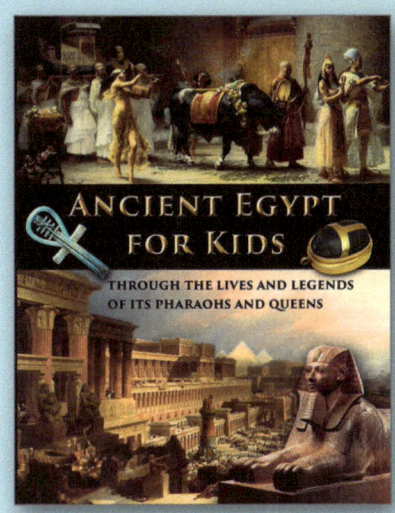
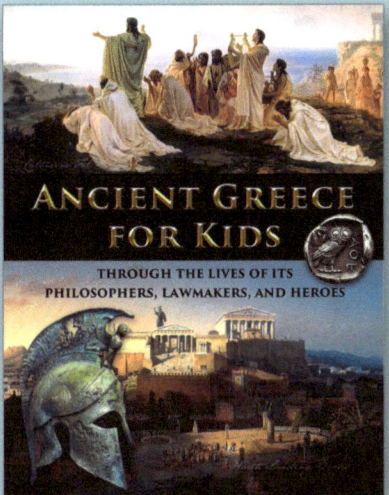
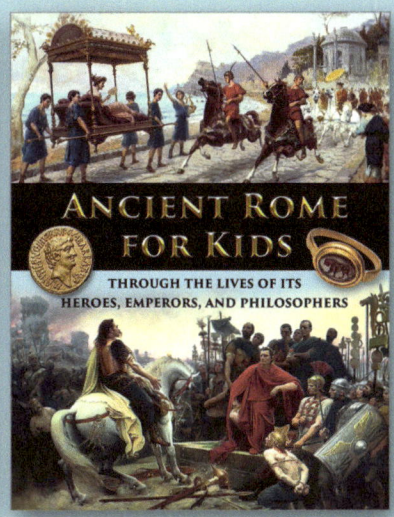
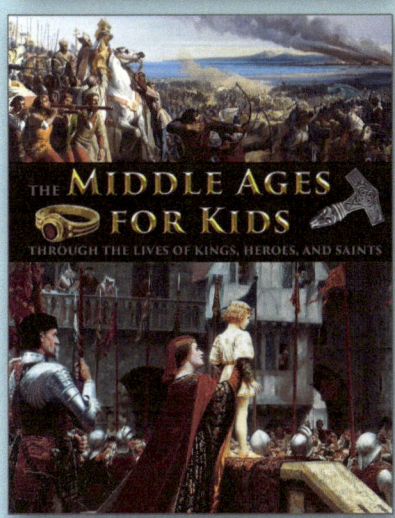
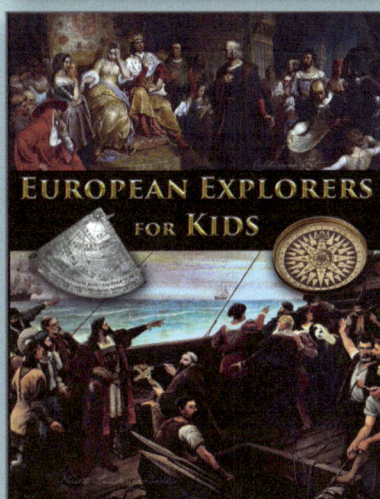
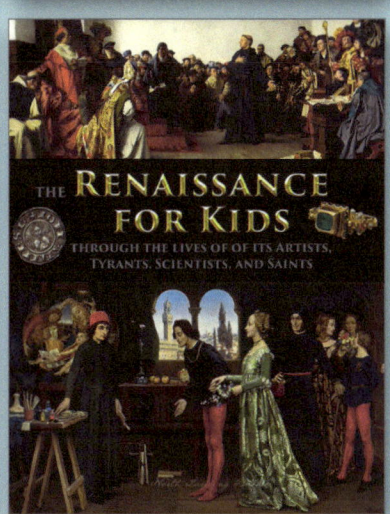
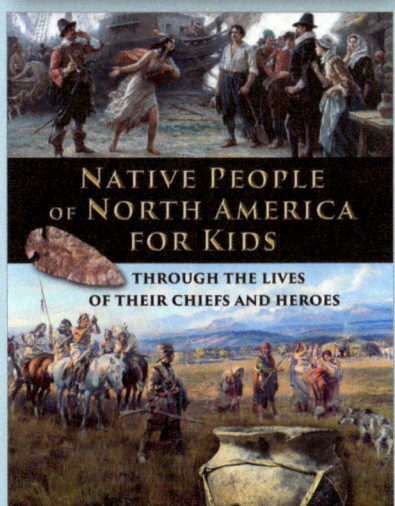
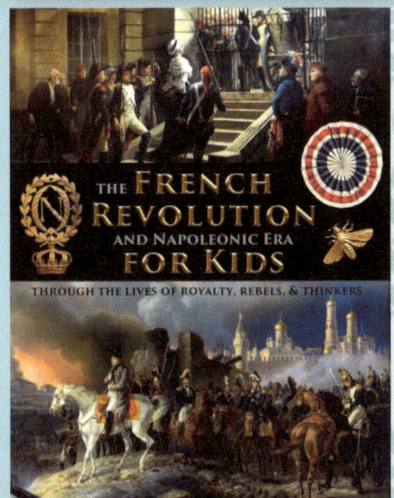
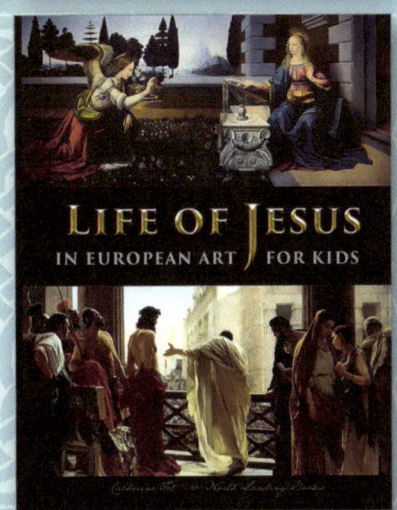

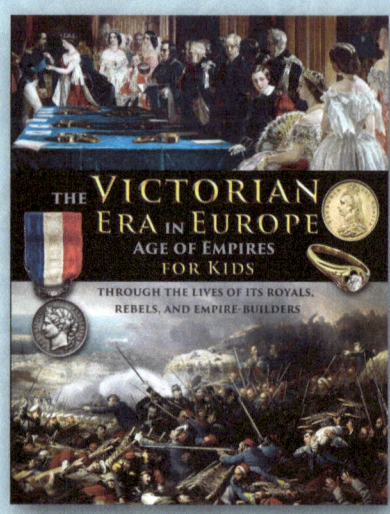
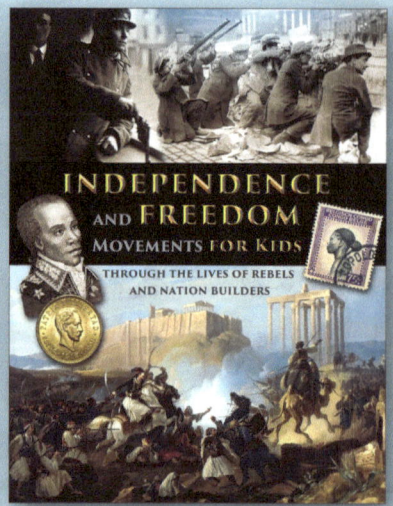
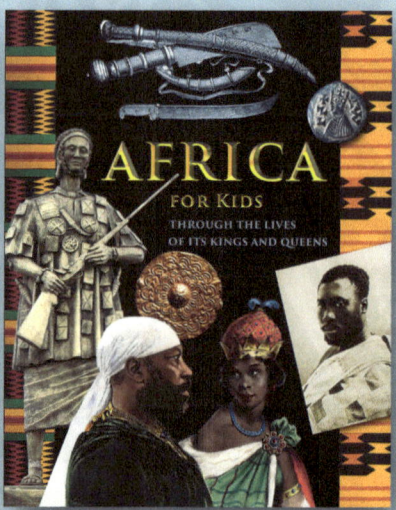
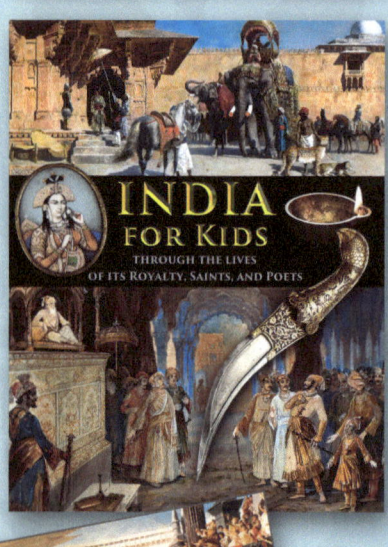
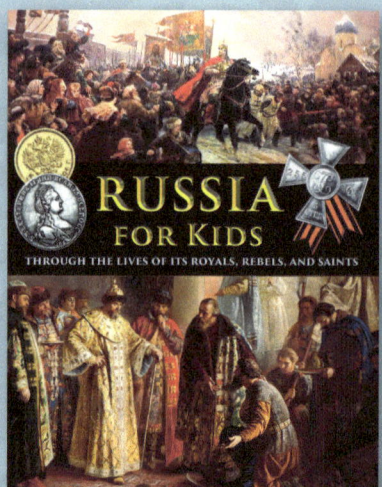

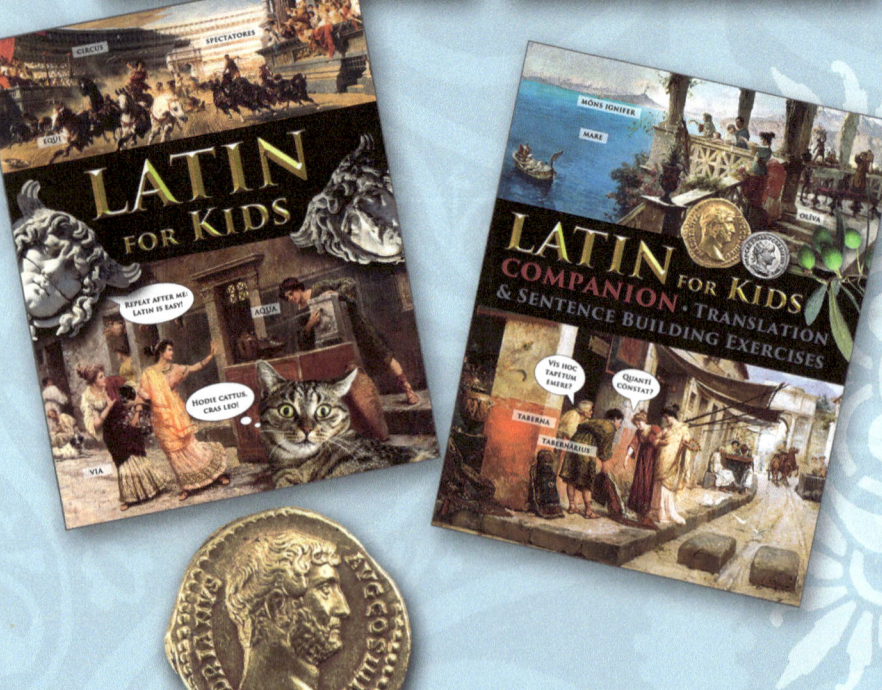

www.ingramcontent.com/pod-product-compliance
Lightning Source LLC
Chambersburg PA
CBHW041433010526
44118CB00002B/62